pardon me, sir

Your
Halo's
Showing

THE STORY OF
J.C. McPHEETERS

by Chilton C. McPheeters

foreword by Maxie Dunnam

Francis Asbury Society, Inc.

Francis Asbury Society, Inc.
Box 7
Wilmore, Kentucky 40390

Francis Asbury's eighteenth century vision was to "preach the Gospel in every kitchen in this country and to spread scriptural holiness over this land." It is the purpose of the Francis Asbury Society to pick up Asbury's pointed challenge in four areas of ministry: *evangelism, discipleship, missions,* and *Christian literature.*

ISBN 0-915143-00-3

To
JULIA
my beloved wife and sweetheart
whose steadfast love, inspiring companionship,
spiritual sensitivity and joyous outlook
have made life with her a glorious adventure
of enduring satisfactions.

Table of Contents

v

Foreword

by Maxie D. Dunnam

One of the big problems of the church is blandness. The flavor of our worship and fellowship is too often as inviting as a bowl of cold oatmeal.

A big part of the cause of this problem is leadership. If the church is "flat," it may be because clergy leadership at the local and national level has been leveled to the lowest common denominator. There are too few eccentrics among us.

Consider the possibility that the question which entered your mind when you read that last sentence (there are too few eccentrics among us) is some validation of my contention that we are plagued by blandness in the church and that leadership has been flattened. The word eccentric, in relation to leadership, provokes questions and uneasy, if not negative, feelings. The word means "departing from conventional custom or practice; differing conspicuously in behavior, appearance, or opinion."

In the most positive way of using that word, this book is about an "eccentric" Christian leader—one of the most effective, colorful, dynamic Christian leaders of this century. J. C. McPheeters' life and witness needs to be remembered, celebrated and modeled.

There is a sense in which the picture that was carried in newspapers across this land—a picture of an eighty-nine-year-old man water-skiing twenty-five miles—is a dramatic parable of who he, Brother Mac, was. He had learned to ski at seventy-three. His whole life was that sort of pioneering spirit, innovative mind, disciplined will, and adventurous heart. An

7

inventive and risk-taking person, he was always on the edge of things seeking to bring the Gospel to bear upon the whole of life. He believed that Christ could redeem every facet of life. This overriding conviction made him a trailblazer. His ministry to farmers in the Ozarks, to tuberculosis patients in Arizona, to prisoners in California; his pioneering work in the use of radio and films in the church and countless other innovative ideas made him a "man of the times."

Yet, he was rooted in the Eternal. Above all, he was a person of spiritual discipline and an ardent preacher of the "timeless Gospel."

His story is thrilling to read—thrilling because he was so powerfully different, but so very much like we can be. His son, Chilton, has done us a service by telling this remarkable story of one of God's noble eccentrics. My prayer is that this story will call us from our blandness and set us on tip-toe, to live our days in the daily affirmation of this servant and saint: "This is the day that the Lord has made; we will be glad and rejoice in it."

Maxie Dunnam, Senior Pastor
Christ United Methodist Church
Memphis, Tennessee

Preface

"Pilgrim Incredible!" My father, Julian C. McPheeters, was born when oxen plowed the fields of Missouri. He wanted to be a lawyer but answered God's call to preach. At age twenty-eight doctors gave him six months to live. His battle for life itself was waged for three long years. JC's adventuring faith then took him westward when highways were marked by painted stripes on telephone poles.

Ambassador for Christ, he served God and humanity as evangelist, pastor, seminary president, religious editor, radio pioneer, and staunch advocate of social justice. For JC, life was always open-ended, a continuum offering opportunity for growth and innovative response. At seventy-three he learned to water-ski in order to keep up with his grandchildren. At eighty-five he had visited all the continents of the world and had traveled a million miles in his thirty-six Chrysler automobiles.

Physical and spiritual fitness were matters of regular discipline. The McPheeters day always began at 4:00 a.m. with a series of strenuous exercises. Following a cold bath, he read his well-worn Bible and prayed. Promptly at eight o'clock his deep voice announced in joyous tones: "This is the day the Lord has made! Let us rejoice and be glad in it!" Until age ninety-four he remained an unrepentant optimist.

I deem it my privilege to have been given the opportunity to write my father's biography. Care has been taken to let facts speak for themselves and to "tell it like it is."

9

Pardon Me, Sir

It is unfortunate that this project was not started twenty years ago when more associates were alive to contribute to the tale. But this in no way alters the factual data. That this story has finally surfaced is largely due to Dorothy Rose, who was for many years Dr. McPheeters' personal secretary. It was her offer to bring together and organize certain personal files that got this task under way two years ago. My personal thanks go to her and to the many others who found time to share their insights and experiences.

I am especially indebted to Dr. David McKenna, president of Asbury Theological Seminary, for making the resources of his office available in the preparation of the manuscript for publication. As a result, I have had the benefit of Dr. Harold Burgess' invaluable expertise and wise counsel in ways too numerous to document. A fabulous support system of trained personnel under the leadership of Dr. David Gyertson, vice president of Seminary Advancement, has helped in a variety of ways: from word processing to proofreading; from secretarial help to the use of computer information banks. Those who have helped in this process have included: Fran Price, Sheila Lovell, Bobbi Graves, Dr. Richard Sherry, Linda Selby, Paul Southgate, Carolyn Smith, June Eisemann, Virginia Fralick, Judianne Lesniewski, Chris Douglas, and Mary Ann Boggs. Although these, and many others not named, have contributed, I accept full responsibility for the final product since any editorial changes were with my consent.

Chilton C. McPheeters
Redwood Christian Park
Boulder Creek, California
April 1983

Postscript

Ten days after this manuscript was completed, my father was immobilized by a stroke that affected the left side of his brain. He had just gotten behind the wheel of his car following dinner in a local restaurant. More than two hours passed before a police cruiser stopped to investigate.

Later, in the intensive care unit of St. Joseph's Hospital, the attending physician shook his head. Given his age and circumstances surrounding his stroke, it seemed unlikely that JC would live long enough to be moved to a private room.

However, Dad's superb physical condition confounded the experts. Paralyzed on the right side and unable to speak with clarity, he, nevertheless, battled back with his usual indomitable spirit and determination. A heroic battle was waged for six and a half months. But the hoped-for recovery was not to be. At the age of ninety-four, coronation day for Julian C. McPheeters had arrived.

The life of Julian McPheeters stands as living evidence of the abiding relevance, dynamic power, and enduring satisfaction inherent in the Gospel of Jesus Christ. The hope is that his example will provide encouragement for others to "taste and see." If persons in an honest quest for truth, righteousness, and peace can encounter this life and say, "Here is a pathway worthy to be explored and embraced by pilgrims who covet the highest and best for humanity," then no one can ask for more.

Pardon Me, Sir

He had fought the good fight.
He had kept the faith.
He had finished the course.
A crown of righteousness was his.

Chilton C. McPheeters
Wilmore, Kentucky
October 31, 1983

Train up a child in the way he should go: and when he is old, he will not depart from it.

(Proverbs 22:6, KJV)

1

The Early Years

A Farm on Logan Creek

The Ozark hills of southeast Missouri is a region some affectionately call "Lappland"—the place where Arkansas laps over into Missouri. Logan Creek in Ripley County lies in the heart of this region. Pioneers found here a welcome land of promise. An abundance of wild game, clear streams and stands of virgin timber provided the material resources needed for homes, barns, fencing and fuel.

Each new household had to clear the land, uproot the stumps, and declare war against each year's invasion of weeds that threatened to reclaim cleared acreage for its own. Those who came, however, relished the challenge and its inherent opportunity to be free, independent and self-sufficient.

Our story begins two decades after the Civil War, when America had made peace with itself. As a border state, Missouri had known the deep bitterness and animosity that divided households and communities over the question of slavery. During the war, members of the same family often fought on opposite sides. Such a legacy brought with it a harvest of festering anger, frustration and hatred. It made the task of reconciliation and healing more difficult than the restoration of damaged buildings.

Somehow the folk along Logan Creek had found a way to forget and forgive the past, evidenced by a community sense of unity, neighborliness and compassion. No better proof of this could be offered beyond the fact that Baptists and Methodists, so often antagonists, lived and worked together as fellow Christians. Unable to afford full-time pastors, they gave reciprocal support to each other's services on alternate Sundays, even extending it to include revival meetings. In many ways they sought to put into practice Jesus' second great commandment to "love your neighbor as yourself." With it came a quality of life and human values beyond the power that material resources alone could provide.

William Garlin McPheeters had spent nineteen of his twenty-seven years in the area when he married Pheriby Edna Greer on July 11, 1886, the bride's eighteenth birthday. The wedding took place under a brush arbor on Cyprus Creek. They established their home in a newly-built house on Logan Creek with eighty acres of wooded land just seven miles east of Doniphan.

The birth of Julian Claudius, July 6, 1889, was an occasion of dual joy for the parents. Not only did his arrival help fill the void created by the death of a fifteen-month-old daughter; a son would, in time, provide needed manpower for the farm. His parents apparently named him Julian Claudius solely for its pleasing phonetic quality. Although Edna Greer had a better education than most women of her day, even writing articles for religious publications, she was unaware of the historic origins of the names selected for her son. It seems paradoxical that Julian, the last great Roman Emperor to seek the revival of paganism and the extermination of Christianity, should have a namesake who would espouse with equal vigor the cause of Christ. However, I never knew my father to use his given names to refer to himself. Always it was "J. C. McPheeters." For this reason I have taken the liberty of using JC as a practical substitute for his given names, at least most of the time.

Perceptible changes had taken place in the life of the nation in the post Civil War years. Farmers began to replace log cabins with frame houses, and mules replaced oxen; the magnetic appeal of urban life began to captivate and lure increasing numbers from the farm. In 1890, the country officially marked the end of the American frontier. The vitality of a slumbering giant was turning toward the goals of an industrial society.

Communities like Logan Creek provided a network of mutual

respect and compassionate response to human need. Friends willingly planted and harvested the crops of a sick neighbor. Volunteer work teams moved quickly to replace, sometimes in a single day, a barn or a home consumed by fire. No challenge seemed too great, no task too difficult, no deed too small in the cause of human succor. Privilege and responsibility remained inseparably intertwined.

"Good Old Days"

If life on the farm was not easy, neither was it harsh by the standards of that day. No one needed to suffer from cold or hunger. The food was varied, ample and nutritious. The menu often reflected the skill of the hunter, with the regular appearance of rabbit, squirrel, quail, wild duck, venison, wild turkey and fish.

Manpower demands, however, were enormous if a family farm was to be truly self-sufficient. William Garlin McPheeters, for example, had to clear forty of his eighty acres for cultivation, land for the family garden, orchard crops, wheat, oats and grazing.

All of this was, of course, a mere prelude to plowing, planting and harvesting. And then there was the torturous ordeal of cutting and clearing the annual crop of spring sprouts, a form of agony and suffering known only to those who have shared in such a maintenance program. One day when JC was engaged in this distasteful task, a neighbor passed by and called out, "Keep it up, my boy, it will make a man out of you." If true, thought JC, then the price was outrageously high.

Farm tools were still simple and, except for the plow, hand-operated at the turn of the century. The cost in human energy was enormous. Harvesters used the hand-cradle for wheat and oat crops. Farmers split rails for fencing by hand, and families had to cut mountains of wood to meet the daily needs of a cookstove and two fireplaces, as well as supply hot water for the weekly laundry and the Saturday night bath. Small wonder that sons were a welcome addition to any farm family.

The daily chores of drawing water, feeding the stock, gathering eggs, milking the cow and conveying food to and from the springhouse seemed like child's play by comparison. At the end of the day no one went to bed hungry, and juvenile delinquency was unknown.

For a farm boy, learning to plow had all the excitement and adventure that learning to drive a car has for today's youth. It marked a transition from boyhood to young manhood. When that great day dawned for JC, his father hitched the plow to a mule, which was slower moving than a horse. With reins knotted and thrown behind the driver's neck, his hands firmly grasping both plow handles, and his eyes fixed on a distant point, JC's first lesson in plowing began.

Plowing a furrow straight and deep is no easy task. It demands patience, perseverence, stamina and strength—a true test of the human will. As the smell of rich soil, freshly turned, permeated the atmosphere, it brought with it a sense of achievement and well-being for JC. Pride welled up within him with the realization that a well-plowed field was one sign that JC was entering adult life and growing responsibility.

Life on the McPheeters' farm was not all work. At noon on Saturday a boy was free to take his dog and go fishing, skinny-dip in the old swimming hole, or hunt rabbits. The standard juvenile equipment for a rabbit hunt was a dog and an axe. The dog first would chase a rabbit into a hollow log. The young master, examining the depth of the log, would chop a hole just back of the trapped animal. It was then a simple task to reach in, grab the rabbit by the hind legs and finish it off with a blow behind the ears. It was a proud young hunter who would return home with more than one rabbit for the family larder.

Allowances for children were unknown. Instead, a father would assign each child a small plot of ground to be cultivated and harvested for personal use. It was a system providing both spending money and at the same time teaching useful lessons about the value of money and the merits of honest toil.

Popcorn was one of the most promising of cash crops, and JC planted and harvested popcorn for his personal use. During the winter months he could earn additional money by trapping quail and selling them at the local market for ten cents each. To increase his catch, JC devised an ingenious pyramid trap that he could bait with grain and a nubbin of corn in such a way that an entire covey might enter the trap before the trigger was sprung. There were occasions, however, when his catch was needed to supplement the family diet.

If farm life imposed heavier burdens on sons, there was also greater freedom to share in the monthly farm-to-market trips. Although these excursions were important for the sale of farm products and the purchase of such needed commodities as sugar and salt, nothing compared with the excitement it generated in a growing boy. Five miles away at Oxley, a branch line of the railroad provided short train rides for five cents. Neeleyville, eight miles from home, was even more exciting with its factory and timber mill.

On very special occasions there was the magic of a two-day trip to the city market in Poplar Bluff, twenty-five miles away. It was an arduous journey requiring an early start one day and a late return on the second day. Sleeping accommodations were under an open sky in the wagon or on the ground. But such hardships were nothing compared with the thrill of steam trains, racing fire engines and the wonders of the local zoo.

Country life was not all toil and drudgery, even for adults. A variety of activities brought people together and enriched the quality of life. Sunday was a day for rest, worship and modest forms of recreation. Church meetings were enlivened by dinners-on-the-ground, brush arbor revival meetings and river baptisms. Then quilting bees, "barn-raisings," family picnics, harvest times and canning sessions brought people together. Later, when threshers and their fire-eating machines began to invade the countryside and take over the harvest, a boy's excitement knew no bounds.

Life, of course, had its hazards. Diseases which have since been overcome at that time took their toll of human life. German measles claimed the life of JC's mother when he was twelve. Rabid dogs were a constant community problem. Shortly after a playmate had been bitten and suffered an agonizing death, JC almost came to the same fate. Fortunately, his father was nearby and able to kill the animal and prevent a similar tragedy. Rattlesnakes were another persistent peril. One memory that remained vividly alive with JC until his death was the time he emerged from a watermelon patch, a melon under each arm, and brushed his bare leg against a rattler. He dropped his melons and with a piercing yell leaped to safety.

Other dangers were associated with life on a farm, from the distemper of a bull to the kicks of a cow or a horse. But none was more strange than that posed by an old gander with a disposition to fight. He would grab a cow or horse by the nose and hang on with his bill, beating it all the while with his hard wings, until the animal could run and buck enough to finally dislodge his tormenter.

One day while a visiting playmate walked through a pasture, this fighting gander rushed to attack him. Running to escape, the boy stumbled and fell flat on his face, breath knocked out and temporarily unable to move. The old gander hopped on his back, biting and beating the lad with those hard wings until it was driven off by a farm hand. By that time the boy's shirtless back had sustained enough damage to turn it black and blue for days to come.

Most families in those days kept a rain barrel at one corner of the house to collect soft rain water. One day JC's six-year-old curiosity got the best of him, and he tried to climb up and see for himself how much water the McPheeters barrel had collected. In the process, he lost his balance and fell in head first. Providentially a neighbor, "Aunt Polly," happened to see him tumble in. She saved him from drowning by yanking him out of the barrel by his heels.

Triad of Community Leadership

For decades in America, preachers, teachers and doctors wielded the dominant influence in rural community life. Not only did their communities consider them indispensable, but they served as inspiring examples of unselfish service and ethical integrity.

Moral leadership, by common consent, belonged to the preachers. Nothing they did was more important than preaching. They preached with great earnestness, marked by a deep concern for souls lost in sin. They preached for an immediate verdict, inviting prodigals to return to the Father's house: "Now is the day of salvation." As a result, sinners were converted, the church edified, and the environment of community life enhanced by occasional renewals of godliness, sobriety and compassion.

The one-room school, staffed by a single teacher, usually stood alongside the church. The six-month school term opened on the first Monday of August and ended in February. Courses included the basics of reading, writing, arithmetic, and grammar along with United States history. Each day began with the reading of a passage of Scripture followed by prayer. The highlight of the week came on Friday afternoon with a spelling bee, a contest that generated intense student interest and keen competition.

Doctors, those stalwart guardians of public health, were accustomed to making house calls around the clock and in all kinds of weather. The most common health problems were measles, mumps, rheumatism and "the chills." The mere arrival of the doctor had therapeutic value. When he opened his black bag filled with pills, powders and liquid nostrums, fear and uncertainty all but vanished. There was a comforting reassurance in the basic rituals of determining fever, lung congestion, ear and throat infections. The doctor was a friend who not only came to dispense medicine, but to share life's experiences and leave behind a message of hope.

The family unit fully supported this triad of community leadership. Nowhere was this more evident, or more necessary, than in the field of religion. Spiritual injunctions were basically taught by living example. The impact of the home in the realm of ideals and values made it the keystone in the arch of society.

Seating arrangements in church separated the men and the women, a strategy intended to make for a better concentration on spiritual matters. An exception, however, was made for courting couples. They were permitted to sit together on the women's side of the aisle while the young lady held her suitor's hat on her lap. They may have been the only persons in the congregation who felt the usual sermon of an hour was not long enough.

The McPheeters family brought from its Scottish homeland a staunch Presbyterian faith, so deeply embedded that it would take three generations to formally join any other denomination. This, however, did not diminish their regular participation in the church life of both the Baptists and the Methodists, the only options open to them.

The Bible was understood to be the word of God for the whole of society. Fathers took seriously the biblical injunction to be the spiritual head of the household. Grace at meals was a common practice both before and after meals. In the evening the family would gather around the hearth and close the day with Bible reading and prayers.

The main facets of Sunday observance were rest and worship. These underscored the heavenly meaning and direction of life. Prohibitions on unnecessary work and secular activities were considered legitimate ways of demonstrating a corporate reverence for God and human worth.

The McPheeters family and others intended Sunday restraints and celebrations to be symbols of gratitude and devotion to the Almighty. They firmly believed in "a sabbath made for man" rather than "man made for the sabbath." In the McPheeters family rough play such as running, wrestling and jumping was forbidden. Equally inappropriate were such things as fishing and gathering wild grapes or huckleberries. Cooking, too, was kept at a minimum. Music and laughter were common as families gathered to sing hymns, tell stories and reminisce. Long walks to the cemetery were also deemed appropriate.

Families considered rules and discipline a necessary and wholesome part of daily life. Violators could expect sure and swift punishment, for parents took seriously the biblical admonition: "He who spares the rod hates his son, but he who loves him is diligent to discipline him" (Proverbs 13:24).

JC often recounted vivid memories of the time he ignored prohibitions against frolicking in the cold waters of the family spring. One hot day, thinking that his father was gone, he stripped down to his birthday suit and entered the forbidden stream. In the midst of enjoying this exotic pleasure, a stern-faced father appeared on the scene, switch in hand, to administer a dose of "hickory tea" intended to erase the memory of the fun of such disobedience for all time to come. And, in retrospect, the strategy succeeded.

"Papa, I Gave My Heart to Jesus"

JC's father, William Garlin McPheeters, records that he had grown up finding great pleasure in always trying to do what was right and avoiding every evil possible.

"I never attended a dance," he wrote, "never went with other boys to steal watermelons, apples or turnips. But on the contrary, I took great delight in visiting the sick of the community." Once he let a friend induce him to drink two drams of whiskey. The state of intoxication and hangover which followed caused him to take a vow, never broken, not to touch liquor again. He lived under the influence of devout parents and helped maintain the family farm up to the time of his marriage.

It came as no surprise, therefore, when the elder McPheeters, feeling God's call to preach, announced plans to sell the family farm. They would move to Fairdealing, where he could enroll in the academy and pursue the necessary studies for qualifying as a supply pastor in The Methodist Episcopal Church, South. Since his conversion in 1884 he had served in the office of class leader, a position that granted him authority to conduct prayer meetings and class meetings and exhort the church to a higher plane of Christian living. He needed, however, a better education to qualify as a local preacher and be able to serve under the appointment of a presiding elder. A year of schooling at the academy would qualify a candidate to become a self-supporting supply pastor. This was one of the ways the Methodist church could keep pace with the spiritual needs of rural America and serve those living in remote and difficult circumstances. It was a role William McPheeters would faithfully fulfill for almost fifty years.

The Methodist church in Fairdealing not only had a full-time pastor, but a building with a tower and a bell so large it could be heard a mile away. Here the faithful gathered to worship God, socialize and sing such favorites as "Amazing Grace," "O Happy Day That Fixed My Choice," and "On Jordan's Stormy Banks I Stand."

In Methodist circles a service of worship often closed with a kind of "Love Feast." Moved by the Spirit, the preacher would invite all who loved the Lord and were in love with their neighbors to come forward, shake his hand and greet each other. It was a touching moment for the participants. Often it elicited emotional shouts of praise and thanksgiving and provided a wholesome catharsis for many.

One Sunday morning, just prior to JC's sixth birthday, the service closed with such an invitation. The message had progressed with more than its usual fervency, making the setting appropriate for a time of friendly handshakes and joyous expressions, but an occasion for adults only. Parents who went forward left their children in the pews.

That day as JC observed the unfolding spectacle he felt a strange warming of his heart and an inner compulsion to give his life to Christ. Audaciously the little lad moved out of his pew and toward the milling crowd at the front. Unobtrusively he joined the company of elders, only to be ignored, unable even to attract the attention of his parents. From an adult perspective his presence there would be regarded as childish curiosity.

Later JC approached his father and said, "Papa, did you see me go up today while they were shaking hands?" "No, my son," was the rejoinder, "I did not see you." "Well Papa, I went up and gave my heart to Jesus." His sensitive father, deeply moved by these words, gathered his son in his arms, kissed his cheeks, and affirmed the good way of life he had chosen in giving his heart to Jesus.

It was a moment never to be forgotten by parent or child. Few experiences would ever surpass these brief moments in the arms of a discerning and Spirit-filled father. From this time on the reality and presence of God would remain inescapably real and personal. The moment had laid a foundation for faith and trust which the severe tests in later life could not shatter.

Six Pennies and a Few Apples

At the tender age of six, JC felt God's call to preach, and with it an immediate sense of urgency. For a six-year-old boy this meant a place to preach protected by secrecy. The perfect solution for JC was to go deep into the woods and face a congregation of trees. This provided the time needed to develop sermons about Joseph, David, Daniel, Jonah and others, laced with generous portions of childish imagination.

Confidence and a decision to "go public" came after a period of time. He rounded up his playmates and informed them that they were to be his congregation. While they heard his announcement with gleeful humor and robust enthusiasm, JC planned no trivial, fly-by-night operation. From the ranks came a song leader and ushers to take up an offering, and from JC, a sermon delivered with earnest zeal. And at the close of the initial service the neophyte preacher was pleasantly surprised to receive six pennies and a few apples for his honorarium. Perhaps no future offering brought more joy or satisfaction. Such peer response was a great encouragement.

JC's fame as a preacher had spread by the time the school year opened. School recess offered a golden opportunity for a larger congregation, a fact that JC was quick to exploit with phenomenal success. Trouble developed, however, when services began to extend beyond the time given for recess. Making the entire student body late for class was not something a teacher would tolerate. The teacher threatened to end JC's preaching career then and there if his sermons were not shorter. He learned the lesson well, remembering the blessings of brevity and respect for time constraints for the career ahead.

This childhood preaching came to an abrupt halt following a near-fatal accident. One late summer day JC went to meet his father as he returned from the lower pasture with the family milk cow. To satisfy his young son's wishes, JC's father dismounted from his horse and lifted him into the saddle for an initial riding lesson. Nearing home, the horse suddenly lunged forward and raced for the barn. The incident might have served only to scare the young rider had it not been for a sharp turn in the road. At this point JC was catapulted out of the saddle, landing head first on the hard ground. Unconscious for over an hour and delirious throughout the night, it was several days before he fully recovered.

The major effect was the end of his childhood preaching. To those who questioned this decision he simply replied, "The horse threw me and knocked all the preach out of me."

Moving to the City

JC was twelve when his mother died of German measles. As a result of her death, life on the farm with three small children became increasingly difficult. More importantly, he would soon be eligible for high school, but the area had no high school for him to attend. The McPheeters family shared America's unshakable confidence in the power of education. At the turn of the century a high school diploma qualified a person to enter the distinguished profession of teaching. The time had come once again for the McPheeters to sell the family farm and move on. This time it would be to Poplar Bluff, which recently had established a high school for their community.

Moving to the city offered a whole new panorama of challenges and opportunities. Foremost, of course, was how well JC could compete with peers whose school year had been much longer. After numerous tests JC entered the sixth grade—the youngest member of his class.

The summer prior to graduation from high school Julian found work in the local spoke mill. He earned ninety cents for a twelve-hour-day as a floor sweeper. Considered too young for the arduous work of an adult, he nevertheless took advantage of every opportunity to observe and ask questions about the work. Soon he was given brief periods of apprenticeship by men wanting a rest break.

Later, when a worker failed to show up, the plant foreman invited him to step in as a temporary replacement. The job was so difficult that men worked all day bathed in perspiration. Even so, young McPheeters carried his work load like a man. When the absentee worker did not return, JC inherited the job for the rest of the summer, and his pay increased to one dollar and thirty-five cents a day.

At summer's end JC, with his newly acquired wealth, was able to visit the World's Fair in St. Louis. Here his vision of the world greatly expanded. He saw his first automobile and discovered the growing wonders of the industrial age. He returned home to find himself quite an authority among his peers. Life never seemed better or the future more bright.

I heard the voice of the Lord, saying, "Whom shall I send, and who will go for us?" Then I said, "Here am I! Send me."

(Isaiah 6:8, KJV)

2

Answering the Call to Preach

A Divine Summons

In the spring of 1908 the young McPheeters was confronted with the question of what to do about God's clear call to preach. The previous summer a cousin, who was a ministerial candidate, had returned home to work in the community. The cousin's human qualities and athletic ability shattered certain stereotypes that JC had about the clergy. Probably to postpone a final decision, JC decided to accept a summer job offer from the Palmer Factory. His task would be to inventory a timber stand of 225,000 acres stretching down into Arkansas. The company would provide a salary of $45 a month and a horse—a handsome sum for those days. It seemed ideal for one who loved the outdoors. This would provide, as well, more time to think and make future plans. In the end it added one more complication: the company was so pleased with his work that JC was offered a permanent job.

Eventually settling in his mind that one must "obey God rather than man," JC enrolled in Marvin College, a Methodist institution in Fredericktown, Missouri. He became a starting member of the football team, captained the baseball team and engaged in track. He also excelled as a member of the school's unbeaten debate team. As a student of Greek, he did so well that the college eventually asked him to teach.

Yet the importance of all these worthwhile activities would pale beside the spiritual impact of the most significant discovery Julian would make as a student in this school, a discovery that would serve as the plumb line for his mission in life.

The More Excellent Way

The Christian college, as an American institution, had been born out of the need to broaden the doors of educational opportunity and, at the same time, strengthen and deepen an understanding of Christian ideals and principles.

At the turn of the century, the fall revival was still an indigenous part of most Methodist educational institutions. It was considered natural to inventory annually the claims of Christ and reinforce the ideals and standards of a biblical faith. The wholeness of life needed both a trained mind and an enlightened faith. Marvin College stood in the vanguard of such a tradition.

In the fall of 1908, for the first time, the shadow of Asbury fell across young McPheeters' pathway. A student by the name of Green had transferred from Asbury College, lured by the availability of a preaching circuit. He was a shocking example of religious emotionalism, daring to punctuate chapel services with an occasional loud "Amen." Green's evident honesty and sincerity commanded the respect of his fellow students who generally agreed, "He is a good fellow, but awfully religious."

One Monday, at the start of the fall revival, Green returned to the campus from his circuit brimming with even more than his usual enthusiasm. He went immediately to the room occupied by JC and his roommate, Jack Wright, with a startling announcement. "I have met the most wonderful Christian on the train ride home, and she has a tremendous experience. I have made arrangements for you two to accompany me to the home of Sister Winter and meet this marvelous woman."

Stony silence and a rising resentment greeted the invitation. It took all of Green's persuasive powers to gain a lukewarm acceptance. Like Wesley at Aldersgate, JC kept his life-changing appointment grudgingly.

The lady in question turned out to be Miss Margaret Skinner, the first deaconess in the Southern Methodist Church. Retired in St. Louis, she had heard about the revival. She had traveled the 150 miles at her own expense in order to hold cottage prayer meetings to undergird this effort. Her countenance alone was convincing evidence to Julian that this dear lady "has something I do not have."

Soon after conversation started, Miss Skinner asked a key question: "Do you believe in sanctification?"

Julian replied in all honesty, "I don't know whether I do or not; you'll have to tell me what you mean."

Quietly this saintly woman began to explain the life of abounding love for God and all His children. She spoke of a victory over sin and evil, and the joy of loving God supremely and your neighbor as yourself. The appeal was to a life of "holiness," understood in terms of wholeness and fullness. She used the term "sanctification" to mean a life of total and unconditional commitment to God and His will. Sanctification became to the life of the spirit what health was to physical well-being. Sanctification meant a balanced and harmonious functioning of the rich and varied facets of life according to Divine intent and purpose.

Miss Skinner went on to read several key passages of Scripture in support of what she had outlined, before pausing for questions. After some minutes of reflective silence, Julian asked, "Is that all there is?"

"Yes," was the bare reply.

"Well then, I will take that right now!"

Immediately an inner voice asked the dreaded question: "Would you be willing to say 'amen' in chapel like Green and have people think you were a fanatic?" It was a salient and crucial question. Full surrender provided the answer of victory.

"Yes, Lord," JC prayed silently, "I will even say 'Hallelujah' if you want me to."

Miss Skinner crossed the room and asked, "Do you believe Jesus sanctifies you?"

"Yes, I do," replied Julian as, for the first time in his life, he clapped his hands in joy and shouted, "Glory!"

The test of Julian's new commitment was not long in coming. The evangelist, in the next chapel service, made a point so valid that he responded with a vocal "amen." The shocked reaction of friends came swiftly. Some gave patronizing reassurance that they understood and would be patient until this temporary emotional fever subsided.

One of his best friends summed it up this way: "McPheeters, we think a lot of you, and you are one of our very best students; but since you have entered into this experience you call 'sanctification' some of us have become concerned about you. We feel you have gotten a little bit off. But we want you to know we are still your friends and believe you are going to be your old self again."

27

As a matter of fact, he never did recover. Doubts might assail, but JC never surrendered or compromised, never turned back. He saw the truth of Scripture, validated in personal experience, demonstrated day by day. Indeed, he found it getting more firmly entrenched with the passing years. Not long before he died, I heard Dad say, "Now as I walk the eventide of life at ninety-three, I can say it is better than ever. It is a life that goes from glory to glory, from victory to victory, from triumph to triumph."

Ozark Evangelism

Some months before JC's graduation from Marvin College, the presiding elder invited him to fill out the conference year at Oran, Missouri. It was a choice preaching opportunity for any ministerial student and, in addition, provided the magnificent stipend of fifty dollars a month. His sermons on the completely dedicated life sparked the greatest spiritual awakening ever seen in the community.

JC's most dramatic and memorable sermon dealt with the moral issue of Sunday baseball, a question that was dividing the community. The subject was: "A Sunday Baseball Game in Hell." It was a natural theme for one who was captain of his college baseball team. The message revolved around the image of the Devil being umpire. JC preached to a packed church, with every member of the baseball team present. Seven members of the team were converted that day, a fact which torpedoed Sunday baseball for the coming summer. This so angered the principal of the high school that he boycotted the church services for several weeks.

When McPheeters' reputation as a preacher spread, invitations to preach multiplied. He turned them all aside, however, for additional academic training, even though his newly acquired Ph.B. was then considered adequate by Methodist standards. An offer to teach Latin and Greek at Meridian College in Mississippi lured him south and provided the coveted opportunity for further study. The new assignment brought him into close association with such outstanding Christian educators as Joseph H. Smith, Frank H. Larabee, John Paul, W. E. Harrison, M. A. Beeson, John Wesley Beeson and his sons, Ralph and Dwight, all of whom would enrich McPheeters' life and remain his lifelong friends.

The greatest lessons learned at Meridian College did not come out of the classroom. Rather, they resulted from a remarkable series of dormitory prayer meetings and the friendship of L. P. Brown, a layman known far and wide as a great exponent of the power of prayer. This man became Julian's role-model for a life of prayer. Seventy-five years later JC still spoke of L. P. Brown as "the greatest man of prayer I have ever known."

Some years later, as JC prepared to close out his ministry in San Francisco, he received from L. P. Brown "one of the most moving letters of my life." What touched him most was a single sentence: "For over twenty-five years I have called your name to God in prayer every morning." It further confirmed one of JC's basic theses: "For much of my success as a pastor I am indebted to this great layman and others like him whom I have had the privilege of working with across the years."

Another crucial decision he faced was whether or not to remain in teaching or to return to evangelism. Storm clouds were gathering in academic circles. Battle lines had begun to appear which could radically alter the meaning and thrust of classical, evangelical Christianity. Destructive criticism had begun to seek to undermine the divine authority of Scripture and reduce it to rationalistic norms. The scholastic challenge and need were there, but McPheeters' call to preach had not been rescinded. "The foolishness of preaching," remained the primary tool for establishing His Kingdom. JC sensed his return to the field of evangelism as inevitable.

His next appointment was, therefore, that of approved conference evangelist for the St. Louis Conference. He selected for his song leader and colleague A. A. Myrick, a converted gambler and peerless personal worker. JC always said that Myrick was "the greatest soul winner I have ever known." Together they made quite a team, turning community after community "upside down" for Christ. Converted sinners filled the Ozark Hills with shouts of spiritual victory and songs of praise. To many it seemed like a reenactment of New Testament times.

Romance and Marriage

"Have Bible, Will Travel" might well have been JC's trademark. He held to a firm policy of never soliciting revival meetings. Even so, invitations far exceeded available dates. The only time JC violated his rule on invitations had unexpected and far-reaching results.

It all began with a Summerville attorney's intense desire to have the team hold a meeting in his home town. With intuitive wisdom the attorney put the matter so persuasively before Myrick, the team's song leader, that he finally agreed to write the church in question and ask for a date. The pastor responded enthusiastically and Myrick set a date to go to this small town in Texas County, eighteen miles from the railroad.

JC received the news and, after a time of reflection, gave his reluctant consent to honor the commitment. However, he made it quite clear that he would not tolerate another violation of principle.

It proved to be a good day's journey from the railroad station to Summersville. Jacks Fork River had to be forded. The road itself was tortuous with steep grades, deep gullies and horseshoe curves. Thick stands of oak covered the hillsides with only an occasional clearing for a log cabin or weatherbeaten frame dwelling. Garden plots and corn fields were monuments of tribute to the herculean toil of the inhabitants. It was a tired and dusty party that finally drew up to the hotel in the town square. On the surface nothing indicated that this would be a date with destiny, that the young evangelist who came to conquer would himself be conquered.

The customary overflow crowd gathered for the start of the revival. For many it was a social as well as a religious occasion. The Chilton sisters made their customary last minute entrance, the epitome of the polished beauty so much admired in that day. They had black hair, brown eyes and peaches-and-cream complexion. Their father, a pharmacist and owner of the local drug store, kept his daughters dressed in the latest styles. Heads turned wherever they went, eliciting stares of both admiration and envy. The young evangelist on the platform was no exception. Incongruously, their appearance injected a very physical note into what was intended to be a very spiritual occasion.

JC lost no time in making discreet inquiries about the Chilton sisters. He was told that one was married, leaving him to speculate and agonize over which one. He inwardly rejoiced when he discovered that Ethel, the girl who had caught his eye, was the unmarried sister.

It takes consummate skill and wisdom to initiate a courtship in the fishbowl environment of a revival meeting. The time available is fleeting at best. And there is the further risk of alienating every other family in the community with eligible daughters who would welcome the same attention. Despite the dangers, Julian established the needed bridgehead for the start of a two-year courtship.

In later years JC took special delight in recounting the perils and difficulties encountered on his frequent visits to Summersville. Rains and floods, ice, mud and snow were obstacles to overcome. On at least one occasion he had to swim the swollen Jacks Fork River holding his clothes aloft in one hand. But with dedication and singleness of purpose he won his maiden's heart. The initial date for a wedding had to be deferred because of the terminal illness of the bride's father. Finally, on January 22, 1914, the wedding took place and the couple departed on a honeymoon that would be shared, as one might guess, with a revival meeting.

The wedding was front page news in Poplar Bluff. The Daily Citizen-Democrat for January 29, 1914, reported in a column headline: "Young Evangelist Returns with Bride." The headline in The Daily Republican had more sensational implications: "Poplar Bluff Minister Weds Convert." And a subheading declared: "Young Wife to Aid Him in Approaching Revival." The lead paragraph read: "Having won her over to that Master whom he is serving, Julian C. McPheeters, a young evangelist of Poplar Bluff, yesterday succeeded in adding personal victory to his spiritual conquest by winning for his own the heart and hand of his young convert, Miss Ethel Chilton."

The life of an evangelist called for gypsy-like living. With no home to call their own, the young couple lived for brief periods of time in a private home or a boarding house. Privacy was at a premium and togetherness all too often involved a crowd. Both needed to give careful attention to what they said. In Palmer, Missouri, for example, the bride happened to mention to her hostess how very fond her husband was of apple pie. For the remainder of their stay a freshly baked apple pie appeared on every breakfast menu.

On the surface this marriage seemed like a most unlikely union. The groom enjoyed the rugged outdoor life of hunting, fishing and camping. The bride had the patrician tastes of a southern belle, more at home wearing the latest styles and enjoying the social graces of a garden party. One was forceful and out-going; the other shy and very much a homebody.

However, because genuine love and affection formed the foundation on which the marriage rested, their differences complemented each other in ways that added strength to their partnership. This country farm boy still needed some of the rough edges honed, and to sense the security and supportive structures of a family life that he had not known since the early death of his mother. This young lady, for whom family and home were central, needed the loving care and protective reassurance of a trustworthy husband.

For the next forty-two years they would journey together, through good times and bad, in sickness and in health, happy in the knowledge that theirs was a love centered in the cause of Christ. Each provided for the other a treasure of support and reinforcement that was basic for life itself. Their earthly pilgrimage together ended on their forty-second wedding anniversary, when Ethel fell victim to cancer.

In *The Herald* of February 29, 1956, a few weeks following his companion's death, McPheeters wrote this tribute: "She served faithfully with me in pastorates of Methodist churches in Missouri, Montana, Arizona and California. In every situation she measured fully to the responsibilities which fell upon her as queen of the parsonage. Her quiet and beautiful life was like the fragrance of blooming flowers on a June morning. She traveled with me extensively over the nation in connection with my work at Asbury Theological Seminary. Although she carried a thorn of physical suffering in her body during the last five years of her life, her faith was triumphant in it all. The last letter she wrote, shortly before she died, was one of consolation and comfort to a sorrowing loved one in the loss of her husband. Her life exemplified in a remarkable manner the way of holiness which she loved. She was beautiful in life and victorious in death."

Early Appointments

Success continued to pursue the young evangelist. However, it became increasingly evident that this sort of itinerary could not continue indefinitely if there was to be any stability for home and family. Then, too, I was born, Julian and Ethel's first child, on February 28, 1915, in the midst of a revival campaign in Poplar Bluff. Mother wanted to name me for my father. But Dad would have none of it. Every person ought to have his own name, he argued. The resulting compromise, Chilton Claudius, bestowed upon me my mother's maiden name, while retaining my father's middle name.

One immediate benefit of my birth was the largest love offering of Julian's evangelistic career. Now, more than ever, JC felt he must take steps to return to the more balanced and stable environment of a pastorate. Once again, however, he felt the need for more academic preparation before making another vocational transition. He went to Dallas, Texas, and enrolled in the newly established Southern Methodist University. It proved a memorable year. Among his classmates were Humphry Lee and Frank Smith. It was also a time when a new strain tested the bounds of faith and prayer. Their infant son became seriously ill and almost died. My survival they regarded as one more miracle of prayer.

After completing a year of study, JC returned to his home conference and was appointed pastor of the Methodist Church in Williamsville, Missouri. Added to his responsibilities was a small church at Leeper. Here a second child, Virginia, was born.

In his second year at Williamsville an invitation came asking that JC be one of the preachers at the next annual conference, a singular honor for a person still in his twenties. Yet this recognition of his stature as a preacher was not without its perils. He strongly felt the urge to use the message God had blessed so abundantly. But the doctrine of sanctification was controversial, and with theological currents flowing in the opposite direction, an unwise choice could easily jeopardize the future of the young preacher. Critics had by now begun to assault this doctrine fiercely, since it could be so easily faulted for emotional zeal and an unloving legalism.

Again, JC felt he had to obey the Inner Voice whatever the personal cost. Preach on sanctification he must. When the time arrived, he preached with great liberty before a capacity congregation and did not hesitate to conclude with his customary altar call. The results were spectacular. How else can one describe an altar filled with preachers willing to seek and tarry for the mighty Baptism?

Before the following day ended, the pastoral relations committee of the Crondolet Methodist Church in St. Louis, later known as Mellon Memorial, began making arrangements to secure JC as their pastor. One major hurdle stood in the way of the appointment. The presiding elder expressed it in a question: "Do you have any hobbies in your preaching?" JC readily admitted that he did give emphasis to the doctrine of sanctification. "But do you make it a hobby?" insisted the presiding elder. "I do not regard that I make it a hobby," came the reply. "But in fairness to you and the church why don't you make inquiry among those who hear me preach and get their opinion as to whether I make this a hobby?" It was not long before the appointment was confirmed.

The move to St. Louis offered further proof that God does bless and prosper those willing to exalt Him and willing to proclaim the total Gospel for the whole of life. It was a day happy with promise.

A transforming spirit of vitality soon quickened the life of the new congregation. Crowds grew and sinners were reconciled to God. But six months into the new assignment a dark shadow fell across the pathway of success. JC's vibrant health and boundless energy now began to give way to fatigue, fluctuating temperatures and night sweats. Five different physicians had prescribed treatment for malaria. JC struggled more and more each week to pull things together for the following Sunday. There seemed to be no escape from the tightening clutches of an invisible enemy that defied even the medical profession. Each week it became more obvious that such rapid physical deterioration could not long continue. Finally, at the suggestion of a friend, he made an appointment to see Dr. Charles H. Neilson.

JC's Fight for Life

In February 1918, Julian entered Barnes Hospital, an adjunct of George Washington University Medical School, and placed himself under the care of Dr. Neilson. It was an act of desperation. Here extensive tests revealed a case of tuberculosis in an advanced stage.

The doctor's verdict was jarring: "You have asked for the truth. There is no doubt, McPheeters, that you are in the final stages of T.B. Both lungs are involved. You have spots on them the size of the palms of your hand. I don't know whether you can be cured. If you had come one month later I would give you no chance at all. As it is, all I can promise is to give you the advantage of every treatment known to medical science. You must give up your pulpit immediately and go to bed for at least six months. In four or five years, if all goes well, you may be able to engage in some kind of light work. You must never think of continuing in the ministry."

Tuberculosis, the dreaded white plague, was as much feared in that day as cancer in contemporary society. What had lurked as a secret fear suddenly became a nightmare reality. JC exchanged a promising career for a battle for life. In that battle, he had the further concern of a family to support and no visible means of income. He dreaded returning home with such grim news. Yet his morale soared at his wife's brave and encouraging response. "We will make this fight and make it to win!" They would enter this valley of the shadow with unwavering faith in the continued providence and goodness of God.

The same dedication and zeal that went into everything Julian did he now focused on the fight for life. At that time, tuberculin injections were the medical profession's main arsenal against T.B. However, JC's recovery would require four other ingredients: a positive mental attitude, fresh air, adequate rest and a proper diet. His Christian faith would guarantee the first; the other elements would be more of a problem.

The initial three weeks of the battle he spent in Barnes Hospital. In the meantime, the church had received their young pastor's resignation and voted to continue him on half salary until the meeting of the annual conference, but the family needed to vacate the parsonage for the arrival of a new minister.

This posed an immediate and pressing difficulty: finding an affordable place to live with a sleeping porch. The only location both suitable and available turned out to be a second floor apartment with an open porch, in a house on a busy street in a decaying neighborhood.

JC left the hospital just in time to help his family move. The exertion involved resulted in a relapse that was nearly fatal. For two weeks his temperature never fell below one hundred and three, and migraine headaches often made him delirious.

About this time a letter of encouragement arrived from JC's father, who had received the news of his son's illness with disbelief. The boy had always seemed so strong and robust, always capable of a full day's work, and superbly athletic. As a man of faith, he put the matter in the hands of God. Retiring to the hayloft, the father had spent a night in prayer, pleading for his son's life.

After the night of prayer, William Garlin McPheeters wrote to his son, Julian: "You appeared in a vision, my son, and I saw your lungs all clouded with spots. Your illness was real and far advanced. You left me and as I prayed on you came again. This time your lungs were clear, my son, without spot or blemish. You are going to get well. You are not going to die." JC held fast to these strong words of comfort and hope. But the road ahead would prove to be both long and tortuous.

Living conditions were barely adequate in the new home. The street was busy and noisy with streetcar lines down the middle. The safety of small children was a constant worry, for the only play areas were the sidewalks and streets. A popular and dangerous pastime for older children was a quick dash out into the street to place a penny or a nail on tracks, to be flattened by an oncoming streetcar. At three years of age, I tried this practice and almost lost my life. Only a quick-thinking older playmate pulled me to safety and saved the family from tragedy.

Medication, diet and rest soon brought signs of slow improvement. JC gained weight, and his condition improved generally. His spirits soared, only to be dampened by the landlord's announcement: he had just discovered the nature of his new tenant's illness, and he wanted no "lunger" occupying his premises. Beginning immediately he would increase the rent fifty percent each month until the family moved.

Financially it now became impossible to stay in the city, even for another month. The only option seemed to be a retreat into the quiet of the Ozarks where costs were lower and neighbors would be more caring. Logic dictated a return to Summersville.

Before the McPheeters family left St. Louis, the local congregation took up a farewell offering as a token of their love and concern. It marked the end of any further Methodist financial support. One church member, however, remembered the family at Christmas for several years with the gift of a twenty-dollar gold piece.

Dr. Neilson's parting advice was to "work at the job of getting well just as you have been working at the job of preaching." Carrying instructions for the local physician, Dr. C. R. Terrell, the little family secured a two-story home in Summersville that boasted a large porch, a good well, and ample room for a garden, chickens, a cow and a horse.

The road to health called for twice-weekly injections of tuberculin. Dr. Terrell charged five dollars a visit to give them at his office, a fee the family could ill afford. To save this princely sum for other pressing needs JC learned to give himself the shots. In addition to the serum, he needed an iron supplement for his blood. Further, to help maintain his energy and promote weight gain, every day he needed fresh eggs, milk rich in cream, and eight to ten hours of sleep.

There was general doubt throughout Summersville that their newest citizen would survive to see the falling leaves of autumn. The contrast between the man of vigor they remembered and the phantom of a man they saw was all the proof required. Years later the local doctor confessed that he, too, held out no hope for recovery. Yet by the time the leaves had turned to red and gold there were unmistakable signs of a miracle.

For encouragement and helpful suggestions, JC and his family avidly read published stories of others who had conquered the disease. One idea JC adopted without any consultation with a doctor. He began to exercise his lungs by exhaling through a small tube as a way to force more oxygen and fresh air into every part of the lungs. The perfect instrument for the task proved to be the stem of a corn cob pipe.

Finally, when his temperature had returned to normal, the doctor allowed JC to start daily walks. He was to begin modestly and then add a few more steps each day until he reached a mile. The major problem he faced was to avoid the temptation of trying to do too much too soon.

Winning the Fight

The urgent need for lots of fresh air made a sleeping porch an important weapon in the battle against tuberculosis. If this was what the cure called for, then there could be no compromise with the weather, as far as Julian was concerned. For over three years he slept on an open porch, even when winter storms covered his bed with snow and ice.

Walking helped him a great deal. Careful to heed the doctor's injunction not to overdo, he celebrated a great day when he reached the coveted achievement of a one-mile walk. This not only indicated a remarkable improvement in his health, but it brought him to the edge of a wooded area which became a milestone. As he extended his daily walk, he penetrated deeper and deeper into nature's wonderland. The chatter of squirrels, the call of a bobwhite and the territorial songs of winged minstrels all had therapeutic value. It was good to stroll on the soft carpet of leaves, to sit on a log and gaze at the towering majesty of giant oak trees, to feel the healing balm of gentle breezes. The ways of nature brought peace to both his soul and body.

Before long enough of JC's strength had returned for him to take down his coveted shotgun and carry it with him. A hunting dog became a necessary companion. Nothing did more to quicken his pulse than the deep bass voice of a Missouri hound pursuing a warm trail. From then on walking had an added practical meaning for the family larder. His good marksmanship provided squirrel, rabbit and other small game in growing abundance.

JC's daily walking schedule exceeded four miles by the winter. The time was right to add a string of traps for marketable animals. Dollars were short, and even austere living did not always stretch them enough to meet basic needs. But dark clouds often have a silver lining. One day the mail arrived with an unexpected checkbook of signed checks. The accompanying note read, in part: "Use these as need arises and know that there are more where these come from." What a gesture of loving concern! It proved an important safety net provided by a man who never became a formal member of any church, but who understood the meaning of the Golden Rule. JC and his family accepted the gift only as a loan to be paid back somewhere down the road, and although that road turned out to be longer and more difficult than imagined, the day came when they repaid it in full.

The winter of 1918 has been known for the epidemic of influenza which swept across America, claiming many lives. JC was fortunate to escape its clutches, since his illness made it doubtful that he could have survived. By the summer of 1919, after almost a year and a half of "chasing the cure," JC felt strong enough to try his hand at selling books and life insurance. In many ways it was easier to sell books than life insurance, but he became so successful that the New York Life Insurance Company made him a very attractive offer to continue with them.

Each new tempting offer of secular employment served only to deepen the conviction that God's call to preach had not yet been rescinded. His doctors, however, continued to advise him against any return to the pulpit for fear of a fatal relapse. But preach he must!

With this in mind, JC returned to St. Louis in September of 1919 for another physical examination and consultation with Dr. Neilson. Although the X rays showed that much healing had occurred, they also revealed that lung spots remained. The doctor strongly advised him to continue his current life-style. However, as if to placate his patient in some way, he gave qualified consent for a cautious and limited attempt at preaching.

Needless to say, it was an elated young preacher who returned home. The Methodist Church in Summersville provided a made-to-order situation for this trial experiment. Lacking a resident pastor, the pulpit was filled on alternate Sundays. JC moved quickly, making arrangements to fill the vacant Sundays.

His return to the pulpit left much to be desired. His initial efforts were feeble when measured by past performances. His weak voice forced him to use a conversational style of preaching with little movement in the pulpit. Indeed, times came when he had to deliver all or part of his sermon while seated. But the passing months brought clear signs of improvement. Then, shortly after the added burdens of the Christmas holidays, he was struck by a near fatal attack of influenza. After a three-week battle in bed, weakened and exhausted, JC could again contemplate the task of preaching.

As summer approached, McPheeters made plans for a revival campaign. The presiding elder agreed to come and do the preaching. The superintendent of the Eminence public schools served as song leader. Even so, the added burden of preparation and the strain of two daily services took their toll on JC. He felt a growing weariness and began losing weight. As a countermeasure he increased his consumption of fresh milk and lengthened his rest periods. The meeting proved to be a great blessing to the community, and JC ended up little worse off for the ordeal.

By the fall of 1920, the preaching schedule had expanded to once every Sunday. Such an achievement was convincing proof that he was ready to resume a full-time appointment. It was a calculated risk whose time had come. In the meantime, he continued his prescribed treatment faithfully.

Agriculture, Education and Religion

Authentic efforts at church renewal have always sought to accent wholeness in doctrine. Francis of Assisi sought it through the vow of poverty. Martin Luther declared it in his great Reformation doctrine, "justification by faith unto good works." John Wesley demonstrated it in a multifaceted program of social outreach. The twentieth century set the stage for a renewed round in this ageless pursuit. JC never doubted that the Gospel must touch and redeem every facet of life. True, he saw the primary task of the church to be that of a spiritual midwife. But the "new birth," like physical birth, was not an end in itself. It must be followed by continued care, guidance and spiritual nurture whose authenticity is ultimately affirmed by an inclusive love and service to humanity. The world doesn't care how much Christians know until it knows how much they care.

As a way to implement this principle, JC had to raise the question: "What can be done for the practical betterment of a rural community?" He found the answer in improved farming. Those on the farm needed to know that it takes more to feed a razorback hog than a purebred; that depleted soil grows less corn; that antiquated methods reduce the rewards of hard work. The marginal productivity of Ozark farms lowered living standards and deprived communities of needed services.

JC's solution was to invite the extension department of the

University of Missouri to conduct a short school of agriculture under the sponsorship of the Methodist Church. The university's response was positive and enthusiastic. Community reaction was less certain. Some, of course, thought the church had no business meddling in secular affairs. Others winked and joked about young "city slickers" coming out to tell farmers how to farm. Yet because of church sponsorship many gave serious attention to the program.

Farmers came from miles around on the appointed day and the church was filled to capacity. Some teachers brought their students. The three-day school closed on a high note of enthusiasm and a request for a repeat performance the following spring. A dozen farmers signed agreements to cooperate with the College of Agriculture in growing kafir corn and soybeans. Pure-bred hogs were introduced. Plans began for the installation of a community-owned lime crusher. It was the start of a new era for land use in that part of the country.

This pioneer partnership of religion, education and farming was written up by A. I. Foard, one of the participating faculty members. His article, "Mixing Farming and Religion," appeared in the March 1922 issue of *Better Farming,* published in Chicago. The effort received high marks and was hailed as a boon to agriculture.

This show of concern for temporal needs and improvements reaped a harvest of benefit for individuals, the community and the church, and caused many townspeople and farmers to abandon their attitudes of indifference and antagonism. The young preacher found himself with a new and growing congregation of seekers. As lives became transformed under the power of the Gospel, the community experienced a growing infusion of Christian love and compassion.

It pleased God by the foolishness of preaching to save them that believe.

(I Corinthians 1:21b, KJV)

3

Maturing Pastor

"Go West, Young Man"

As JC's strength and vigor returned, the time seemed right for resuming a conference appointment. Discreet inquiry brought assurances that there would be an opening for him in St. Louis. Excited about the prospects of picking up where he had left off, JC was present for roll call when the St. Louis Conference convened in September, 1921.

It was a day and age when Methodist bishops exercised autocratic authority over ministerial appointments. Any consultation with pastor or congregation was unnecessary, and even when this took place, the bishop made the final decision. The highlight of any annual conference, therefore, came on the closing night when the appointments were read. Typically, pastors learned only at that moment whether they would return or be moved to a new church.

The prominence of preaching made it customary for annual conference programs to feature a guest preacher of note, most often an episcopal colleague of the presiding bishop. As fate would have it, the guest preacher for the St. Louis Conference was Bishop H. M. DuBose. He was the newest member of the Council of Bishops, having been elected in 1920. According to custom the new bishop had been assigned to the Far West. This vast geographical domain, sparsely populated, stretched from Canada to Mexico. He had come, therefore, not only to preach, but to recruit men to fill vacancies in the Northwest Conference. McPheeters was on his "hit list."

Bishop DuBose called JC for an interview and offered him a church in Missoula, Montana. Despite the glowing picture painted about the challenge and opportunity, JC has reservations about the severity of the climate. The bishop emphatically reassured him that winters in the region were both brief and mild, further moderated by the dryness of the cold. The bishop had been there the previous November and enjoyed a week of salubrious weather. He described the land as a veritable Garden of Eden, with climate unmatched in beneficence for health. The bishop's sales pitch made it seem folly for one in McPheeter's shoes to turn down a situation so ideally suited for all his needs. However, on Bishop DuBose's next visit to Montana he discovered for himself just how salubrious the weather really was—caught away from his hotel and lost in a blinding snowstorm, he very nearly froze to death.

In blissful ignorance, a buoyant JC announced his decision to go west, sending shock waves among friends and colleagues. After a brief round of farewells, he hurried home to calm his wife's mounting distress. With no prior hint of such a radical change of plans, it was only JC's repeated description of the bishop's grandiose picture that could reassure Ethel that all would be well. Then, with the true spirit of an itinerant Methodist preacher's wife, she turned to the task of packing for the long journey and saying good-bye to familiar surroundings and to family and friends.

The Montana Adventure

The anomaly of Southern Methodist churches throughout the Far West was a direct outgrowth of the plantation system of the South. Since the family inheritance normally passed to the eldest son, younger sons often sought their fortunes elsewhere. This encouraged a remarkable migration westward, accelerated no doubt by the discovery of gold in California. Building churches followed as a natural result, especially since Southerners often faced hostility and suspicion by those opposed to slavery.

The Civil War brought this westward migration to a sudden halt. All available manpower was needed to rebuild from the ravages of war. Indeed, a reverse migration took place. Despite such reversals and the need to close down some churches and institutions, a viable network of Southern Methodist churches existed throughout the Western states.

On the morning of October 17, 1921, JC and Ethel's friends and relatives gathered in Summersville for an emotional farewell. It must have been a scene reminiscent of the days of Abraham. A newly purchased Overland touring car stood ready and overloaded. Their leaving this late in the season would make the journey a race against time and the vagaries of weather.

The McPheeters family first stopped to pick up another passenger, the Rev. J. A. Baxter, a ministerial colleague who had agreed to pastor a church in Butte, Montana. Economic necessity dictated they find space for this large man and one suitcase. Ethel and the two small children shared the back seat. The only space for luggage was a built-on luggage rack and the running board on the driver's side of the car. Side curtains provided some small protection from wind and rain.

The Overland automobile undoubtedly improved on travel by wagons and horses, but it still left much to be desired. The highways of the time were designated by colored bands painted around telephone poles. In the open country of the West, travelers had to open and close gates by hand as traffic moved across the vast private ranches of the day. Snow was an ever present danger in mountain passes that late in the season. As they feared, the weather cost them a day in Wyoming as a blizzard passed through the area.

On the final day of the journey, while JC was trying to follow a highway still under construction, the axle of the overloaded car broke under the strain. This kind of accident happened so commonly that many motorists carried a spare axle. The only way to complete the journey now was to flag the night train. However, this posed a financial problem for a pastor whose resources were all but gone. The solution came when a construction worker agreed to a loan of twenty dollars with JC's cherished shotgun held as collateral.

On the first day of November, the McPheeters family finally reached their destination. Many considered their two-week journey a miracle of speed for such a trip. A welcoming committee met the train and took the travel-weary family to their new home.

Missoula was a beautiful city of fifteen thousand people nestled amid snow-capped mountains. Located at the mouth of the fertile Bitteroot Valley, the city was divided by the Missoula

River, which flowed out of Hellgate Canyon. At 3,000 feet, the atmosphere of the city was invigorating and the climate dry. The growing season was short, but prolific. It was a year-round paradise for fishermen. A branch of the University of Montana enhanced the intellectual and cultural life of the community.

The initial two weeks of November, with the warmth and beauty of an Indian Summer, turned out to be all the bishop had promised. However, all this came to a sudden end one night when a full-blown blizzard roared out of Hellgate Canyon, depositing two feet of snow and plunging the mercury below zero. It was May before the ground became visible again.

Local citizens hastened to assure the new residents that the weather was "most unusual." Later, the United States Weather Bureau confirmed this to be the coldest winter in thirty-two years. This was small comfort when JC learned that automobiles normally had to be drained and put up on blocks for the winter season. The citizens depended on public transportation and walking as their modes of travel. When JC took his first walk downtown, his ears almost suffered frostbite before a discerning merchant warned him of the danger. He immediately bought his first fur cap with ample earflaps for protection.

Maintaining family life was difficult. The family had to stoke the coal stoves day and night. The parsonage bedrooms not only had no heat, but the windows could not prevent fine snow from blowing in and onto the floor. JC had to keep a pathway to the nearby school shoveled out and maintained so I could make it to my first grade class.

The task of rejuvenating a dying church presented JC with a staggering challenge. The congregation had lost confidence in the future, was plagued by dwindling resources, and resented the bishop's refusal to honor their request that the church be closed. Undaunted by circumstances, Julian did the one thing he knew to do—proclaim the Gospel of a redeeming Christ. Soon the empty sanctuary filled to capacity as crowds and membership doubled.

The vision of the congregation began to turn outward beyond itself as people experienced conversion and changed lives. A special ministry soon developed to help meet the needs of men in a nearby army fort. Two outpost Sunday schools quickly grew in unchurched communities. Classes began on Sunday afternoons and were staffed by volunteer teachers. One young couple resigned from government service and went to the mission field. JC and Ethel had fanned the embers of a dying church into an exciting blaze of Christian love and service.

As winter passed into spring and summer the countryside indeed became a Garden of Eden. Thousands of acres of blooming orchards perfumed the air. The short growing season produced a rich harvest of vegetables, fruit and flowers. A small boy, like I was then, could pick raspberries and sell them to the corner grocer for twenty cents a pint.

The environment of Missoula proved to be beneficial. The last traces of JC's annoying cough disappeared after a four and one-half year's siege. The cool midsummer nights assured refreshing sleep. From every point of view all seemed well with the world.

Desert Horizons

Well into the second winter another devastating illness invaded the McPheeters family. The victim this time was the wife and mother, Ethel, who contracted pneumonia for the fourth time in her life. The recurrence alone made the disease one of greater peril for her. Pneumonia also was especially dangerous at Montana's high altitudes.

The family physician was Dr. Charles Thornton, a devout Seventh Day Adventist. From a medical standpoint, Thornton held out little hope for Ethel McPheeters' survival. However, as a man of faith and a firm believer in the power of prayer, he frankly expressed his belief that her only hope lay in this direction.

Therefore, Julian sent wires to praying friends across the nation asking prayers for his wife. After some anxious days the crisis passed, and Ethel's recovery seemed assured. But the day of celebration turned out to be premature.

An unexpected and serious complication developed. It was Vincent's angina, commonly called "trench mouth." The prognosis appeared even more grim. For twelve weeks a high fever never left her. Nurses attended her around the clock. Both of the McPheeters children had to go and live with neighbors. The prayer chain continued its ministry of earnest intercession.

As I attended class at the nearby school, I was permitted to come home each school day to have lunch with my father and catch a fleeting glimpse of my mother, who looked the picture of death. Indelibly etched in my memory is the image of my father kneeling by the table at the end of the meal and praying that God might restore my mother to health. As it turned out, she was the only one of six patients afflicted with Vincent's angina who did survive that winter.

Yet there was a price to pay. Another Montana winter could prove fatal. The doctor advised a move to a milder climate. JC lost no time in notifying his bishop and requesting a transfer. The reply was positive. A new church was under construction in Tucson, Arizona, and he would be named its first pastor at the next session of the annual conference.

The trip to the new promised land far to the South would be long and difficult. Instead of "full speed ahead" there was the need to cope with a two-month interval between the Northwest Annual Conference and the Arizona Annual Conference. Included in the problem was the absence of any paychecks. Again it became necessary to borrow money in order to acquire the latest camping equipment: a waterproof tent with a floor, Coleman stove and lantern, a folding table and chairs, and an evaporative cooler that could be fastened to the running board of a car. A custom-built metal rack was also fastened to the back of the Overland to provide expanded space for needed essentials.

Travel by car under these circumstances was considered deluxe. Auto courts, the forerunner of today's motels, were in their infancy. Flourishing public camp grounds, however, offered running water, public showers and rest rooms at a nominal fee. All a family had to do was pitch a tent, set up camp, cook a meal, wash the dishes and get the children ready for bed. It was certainly no easy road for Ethel, weakened by long illness, and not attuned to roughing it in the outdoors.

An unexpected bonus came when the Reverend Mr. McPheeters was asked to supply the Methodist Church in Chico, California, for a three-week period prior to the arrival of a new pastor. This welcome interlude provided needed financial assistance, comfort and rest for our travel-weary family. Finally we were off to Southern California to attend the next session of the Pacific Annual Conference.

Unfortunately, the stay in Southern California did not provide a favorable introduction to Arizona. Many of our acquaintances, perhaps out of ignorance, readily recited tall tales about the perils of desert life. The landscape of burning sands and parched mountains was presented as a miniaturized Hell. The land itself apparently suffered from a hideous infestation of rattlesnakes, scorpions, centipedes and other noxious creatures. The worst horror story, however, focused on the gila monster, a poisonous desert lizard. Someone declared it to have a bite so lethal that it could kill a person in a matter of minutes. Some claimed it had the speed of a race horse and had been known to leap into passing automobiles to claim its victims. Such a piece of fiction could and did send chills down the spine of the bravest traveler. Ethel McPheeters unfortunately accepted these tales as truth; for her they were sure harbingers of impending disaster.

The journey from Los Angeles to Phoenix was a long and difficult one. The most hazardous part of the trip lay between Indio and Blythe, an uninhabited stretch of desert covering ninety-two miles. A single service station was located at Desert Center, about midpoint in the journey. Travelers carried extra water bags, knowing that every drop of water had to be hauled into Desert Center and then sold for the premium price of one dollar a gallon. For the fainthearted it was one more reminder of the risks inherent in desert living, or should one say, existence.

It was a weary and fear-filled family that finally pulled into Phoenix. Like any anxious mother, Ethel was physically depleted by the nervous energy she had expended monitoring desert horizons for anticipated dangers. She would have returned at once to the familiar regions of the Ozarks if that had been an option.

The site of the annual conference was Central Church, the mother of Arizona Methodism, established in 1870, the very year the city of Phoenix was founded. Here in 1923 JC was invited to preach his first sermon in Arizona. Little did he dream that forty-five years later the young boy at his side would be appointed pastor of this historic congregation.

The final stage of the two-month saga began with the adjournment of the annual conference. The road to McPheeters' appointment in Tucson stretched southward for 130 miles. Under ordinary conditions, at that time, the trip could take the better part of a day. Hot desert sands proved to be hard on tires that only had a 5,000-mile guarantee. In retrospect, it takes a certain audacity to look back upon those as "the good old days." Any punctures called for a lengthy ritual of repair, and the McPheeters family experienced five of these rituals on the road from Phoenix to Tucson. The sun was low in the sky by the time they reached their ultimate destination. With a sense of relief and gratitude, a weary family crossed the threshold into their new home in Tucson.

Tucson: "The Sunshine City"

Tucson, with a population of twenty-three thousand, was the largest city in Arizona when J. C. McPheeters and his family arrived in 1923 to begin work. An established health center, the city advertised itself as "The Sunshine City." But the desert landscape seemed harsh and uninviting to JC, who had grown up in a region of clear streams and green forests. Still, the desert lowlands of Southern Arizona abounded with plant and animal life. Mesquite, ironwood, palo verde and greasewood trees mixed with eighty varieties of cacti to form a habitat for a multitude of birds and small animals. The customary winter rainfall assured a burst of flower-cover to celebrate the coming of spring. Sportsmen had seasons for hunting quail, dove, white wing, deer and wild pig.

A special tranquility descended on the desert at dawn and sunset. Against a mountain background, the desert inspired a unique sense of reverence for life and the glories of God's creation. No more spectacular sunsets seemed to exist in any part of the world. At night the stars shone with a brilliance that made them seem close enough to touch.

Tucson had once aspired to be the home of Arizona's State Prison, but this "economic plum" had been given to the competing city of Florence. Tucson had to be satisfied with second best; it was awarded the new university. In 1923 this was still a live issue, though in retrospect few would disagree that for Tucson to lose this battle was to win the war.

It was in this context that, according to the custom of the times, a band of Southern expatriates had petitioned the Methodist Church, South, for help in establishing a new congregation. The presiding elder had investigated the situation. His recommendation to the Church Extension Society was that a new church, the University Methodist Church, South, should be located on a desirable piece of land just four blocks from the main gate of the University of Arizona.

Once again JC began the task of "making brick without straw." Church life centered in a temporary frame building located at the back of the church property. Later, volunteers demolished this structure and its lumber became the floor of the church basement. In the meantime, JC preached the gospel, sinners were converted, and a new pattern of church life began to emerge.

Once the erection of the outer shell of the church, provided by denominational largess, was complete, the responsibility for the building fell upon the members. Eventually the members finished the sanctuary, along with its beautiful balcony. They installed an organ to provide an appropriate environment for worship, and added a front portico with tall white columns typical of Southern architecture. The columns seemed a bit incongruous amid the Spanish architecture of the growing city of Tucson, but they were a nostalgic reminder of home for many of the worshipers as they arrived.

Long standing customs prevailed: Sunday morning and evening services; Sunday school classes for all age groups; multiple youth groups prior to evening services; a midweek prayer meeting on Wednesday night. No summer would be complete without a daily vacation Bible school. And at least one revival meeting was held each year.

Into this standard mix came work days, church dinners, women's meetings, class picnics and other social events to help people get better acquainted and form enduring friendships. The town boasted two Olympic-sized public swimming pools with generous picnic space. The church held annual barbecues at one of these pools and made them red-letter days for all participants.

Proximity to the university made possible the development of an extensive program with a creative and talented group of students who greatly enriched the life of the church. They taught Sunday school, sang in the choir, published their own newspaper, staged musical extravaganzas, called on shut-ins and gave support to projects helping meet community needs. Some would go forth as ministers and missionaries.

A Ministry to Shut-ins

Many of the families in Tucson had moved there as a measure of last resort to meet the health needs of some family member. The majority were victims of tuberculosis. Those who benefited most from the climate were usually persons whose illness was in its early stages.

The needs of these new arrivals were many and varied. First were the needs for adequate housing, medical attention, and employment. They needed friends to help overcome moods of loneliness, depression and despair. Strangers in a strange land, far removed from the familiar ties of family and lifetime friends, they desperately sought sympathy and understanding. It was a formidable task to rebuild the fabric of community support lost by moving away and breaking family ties.

J. C. McPheeters' own victory over tuberculosis made him a walking testimony of hope. It gave him special entrance into many homes and provided him with unique opportunities for inspiring and encouraging others in their fight for life. He felt an urgent desire for the university church to find a way to reach out to more people with this message of faith, hope and love.

Radio was just beginning to come of age. Crystal sets gave way to table and console models whose vacuum tubes guaranteed vastly improved reception. Listening to Amos and Andy was becoming a national pastime. This was motive enough to bring about the purchase of our family's first radio, a Spartan.

JC determined to use this new medium as a vehicle to bring the Gospel to the ill and homebound, and became one of the first to have an active radio ministry. Soon the Sunday morning worship service was being broadcast over KVOA, sponsored by the leading mortuary in town. Of course, some criticized such an arrangement. But his critics could not provide a better alternative. This innovative and radical arrangement proved to be a blessing to a growing and appreciative audience.

Some months later, JC decided to air a ten-minute devotional five mornings a week at eight o'clock. The broadcast would have to originate from the church, in order to take advantage of the studio already in place. JC enlisted other members of the family to help solve one logistical problem of timing. When the station announcer introduced the program by way of the family radio, from the back porch of the house someone would flash a signal to JC, who then had just enough time to get to the microphone. It was a system that worked well for many years.

Such a radio ministry made special demands on Julian's style of preaching. He was no longer free to pace about the platform or give free reign to his vocal powers. Time, too, had to be respected. If this was the prescription needed for an effective radio ministry, then he was determined to be the first to obey its dictates. The experience proved to be valuable training to meet the disciplines of the growing electronic age.

Soon another community need presented itself. The fear of tuberculosis, not unlike leprosy in ancient times, became so universal that its victims became the pariahs of society. As a result, the Tucson Public Library had developed a policy which prohibited any circulation of books among tubercular patients. Thus, those most in need were deprived of the enjoyment and help books could provide. JC's answer was to establish a circulating library for shut-ins.

Twelve teams of two women volunteers blanketed the city every two weeks. They brought with them a car full of books, and carried select volumes and a master list to the bedside. Patients then selected as many volumes as they wanted for a two-week period. This service the church offered without cost to any and all who might desire it.

Through the radio JC invited the general public to contribute books and money for this project. The response was overwhelming. In a matter of days the church received three thousand volumes. Grateful shut-ins called in to have their names placed on the visitation list. For years the program blessed the lives of thousands of persons. And the outreach of these friendly volunteers often opened doors of opportunity for the church to enlarge its ministry in meeting deeper human need.

Another important development came with the establishment of the Southern Methodist Hospital and Sanatorium. Backed by the denomination, it sought to help overcome the acute shortage of adequate living facilities for the victims of tuberculosis. The goal was to provide the best of loving care at the lowest possible cost.

An early advertisement released nationwide declared:

An institution well-equipped for the treatment of all types of tuberculous infections. Sun-porches and roof so constructed that our patients may have full benefit of the sun treatments. Essential consideration is given to the patients' diets. All private rooms; with or without individual sun-porches; with or without private baths. The dry, mild winters are ideal for those suffering from respiratory diseases. Elevation 1500 feet.

The tragedy of illness often compounded itself with the economic necessity for families to be separated. A mother might accompany a sick child to Arizona while the father kept his job and lived at home with other members of the family. Such situations often gave the church a special opportunity to be of service.

An example of this was Julian's pastoral ministry to Dalton Langham. Only twenty-two at the time, Dalton made the move west as a last resort. He and his mother needed a pastoral presence to help face the recurring cycles of hope and despair and the added loneliness caused by broken family relationships. JC became an inspiring role model for Dalton, and a surrogate father at times. But even more important was the Gospel message of love and transcendent hope. After four years it became increasingly evident that Dalton might not live to celebrate his twenty-sixth birthday. Yet the valley of the shadow of death held no fears for Dalton Langham. Acting on a premonition, he declared his faith in a brief bit of verse and placed it in a bedside drawer for a grieving mother to find and read after his death. Dalton had made his peace with God and the world and departed life here without anger or acrimony.

"And what if tonight be the sunset of life for me,
    As long as it be a glorious one?
For tomorrow I shall see the eternal dawn,
    In the land of the rising sun.

What does it matter if I have run my race,
    And my work assigned me is done?
As long as I have looked the world in the face,
    I know I have conquered and won."

At the opposite end of the spectrum were those whose illness lingered on for decades. For twenty-two years Louise Preston seldom got beyond the door of her bedroom. She had to spend much of her time in bed. Yet those who came to comfort left inspired by her glowing faith. Unable to go out into the world, she invited the world to come to her. She developed a global correspondence with persons who were ill, lonely and despondent. She wrote inspiring articles for publication. As a confidante of youth, she encouraged many to give their lives to Christ in full-time Christian service. She seemed to have no time for bemoaning her fate or indulging in the acids of self-pity. Her illness became an altar for service and a channel of God's redemptive grace. And when her eternal summons came, all who knew her could declare, "Well done, thou good and faithful servant of the living God."

It was a kind of tonic for many of Tucson's tubercular patients to spend an hour with J. C. McPheeters. Having shared their suffering, he could ask them to share his faith. Many found new hope and comfort in the midst of affliction, sustained by a faith stronger than death. The story of his life became a healing balm blessed by the Spirit of God.

Practicing What You Preach

The parsonage, located next to the church, was a magnet for people seeking help. Whatever the need, whether financial, shelter, work, medical care, loneliness, or spiritual despair, JC and Ethel made every effort to lend a helping hand. Often their greatest gift was the knowledge that someone cared and was willing to share.

One of the most striking illustrations of this compassion came one day when two teen-age brothers knocked on the parsonage door. They had come from the Midwest to make a new start in life, following the untimely death of both parents. Their immediate need was for housing within walking distance of the university and the high school. JC offered several suggestions and told the boys to return in the event their efforts proved unsuccessful.

There was something pathetic about two orphans trying to take root in a community where housing was at a premium. Ethel's motherly instincts stirred deeply. She and Julian decided that if the brothers returned, and they agreed to the idea, the McPheeters family would offer to rent them a large bedroom on the back corner of the parsonage, which had its own entrance, a private bath and sleeping porch.

Thus did Gordon and John Gordon become a part of the McPheeters family. "Dad and Mother Mac," as the brothers affectionately called them, would serve as surrogate parents, and these expanded ties of family would remain an ongoing blessing. Years later, when the Gordons wrote *The Tumult and the Joy*, a novel about a minister, JC served as one of the role models.

This kind of personal touch permeated JC's ministry and led to the phenomenal growth of University Church. When he moved onto a new assignment, after seven years, he left behind the largest church in the conference.

Invited back, years later, for the fortieth anniversary celebration, he sat down to dinner with over 200 people who had joined the church under his ministry. Many, too far away to come, sent letters of appreciation. The Rev. Maurice B. Cheek, who had served two years on the staff as a youth intern, wrote from California:

> All your labor certainly brought good to many people, especially among the seekers of health. I can remember your driving the old Maxwell from home to home, in hot weather and cold, and you always had a cheery greeting and a word of prayer. Each of your sermons had a personal appeal to accept Christ, trust in God, and follow the leading of the Holy Spirit. I can recall Rubye Milam exclaiming after a meeting in the patio out back . . . "Why haven't we been told before how God's Spirit works?" Then, the Epworth League and the student work . . . leaders like Tom Hudspeth, Florence Wilcox, Ozzie Foster, the Klass sisters, the Van Dorens did such fine youth work. I can recall Easter

sunrise services on the desert . . . drama such as "At the Gate Beautiful" with scenery borrowed from the University . . . people like Margaret Billingsley going to the mission field . . . Louise Preston leading youth into life service . . . revival meetings, the choir, the Women's Society, the Junior League . . . the Vacation Church Schools . . . installing the new pillars in the front of University Church . . . the L. E. Wyatt family . . . the deaconess, Miss Canon . . . how your wife, Ethel, helped keep us organized . . . and how Allie Russell came from Roswell and boarded with the Howell family, and later became my wife . . . it was a busy two years that I valued because you taught me so many things about a church and people and the Christian life . . . it was during your supervision that I decided to become a local preacher. For all this and more I wish to express my appreciation and gratitude.

"The Terror of Euclid Avenue"

"PK" is an abbreviation for "preacher's kid," a special breed supposed to have unique chromosome endowments guaranteeing flawless Christian conduct from the cradle to the grave. Just as doctors were faulted if family members got ill, so, too, were the clergy held accountable for any imperfections or improprieties on the part of their families.

As a practical result, I was forced to live under a double standard of judgment. The mischievous conduct of other children could be brushed aside as normal; for me, as a PK, it was a scandal against the Almighty.

JC was fortunate in having a daughter, Virginia, who was a very paragon of virtue and decorum. She was a docile and obedient child who always made the school honor roll and seemed naturally to do all that parish critics expected of her. To help guard the family sanctity she also felt a special call to help monitor and report the infractions of her iconoclastic brother.

I was called by some "the terror of Euclid Avenue." Others, not so generous, whispered that I would surely "end up in jail or the electric chair." Such a son in the parsonage was, without doubt, a painful cross for a preacher father to bear.

Judged by current standards, the adolescent conduct of the 1920s appears innocuous. Disruptive but seldom destructive, I was mischievous without being vicious. These transgressions included such things as: building a hut to provide headquarters for a secret society, where the most daring thing done was to smoke cigarettes made out of crushed leaves; disengaging a streetcar's power line to delay passengers and create more annoying work for the conductor; raiding the ice truck to gather up discarded ice chips; disrupting Sunday school class with "horse play" while plying the teacher with impertinent questions; and projecting an unrepentant attitude of indifference about what people might think or say relative to conduct.

My father took the Bible seriously and knew what had to be done when periodic reports filtered back to the parsonage about wayward conduct. If "to spare the rod is to spoil the child," then corporal punishment became a heavenly mandate. A mulberry tree adjacent to the front porch provided ideal tools for "loving chastisement." He cut so many switches from this one tree that it almost died from mutilation.

Permissive parents and families run by the whim of children were exceedingly rare. Parents were not in the business of winning popularity contests. Some requirements of conduct were beyond question in every household. Our requirements included regular attendance at church and school, respect for elders, reverence for the Ten Commandments and the Saturday night bath. Most of Sunday was spent at church, which included Sunday school, Epworth League and the morning and evening services.

As PKs, some of us envied those friends whose parents released them from mandatory church attendance. Our task was to endure the best way we could. Singing hymns helped some, and most sermons had a story or two that could capture attention. Other portions of the service we tolerated by reading Sunday school papers carefully tucked between the pages of a hymn book as a camouflage for such irreverence. However, one could do little about an adult prayer meeting except endure it.

The anvil of obligatory requirements can forge a personal faith or serve as an excuse for shattering what faith one might have. Authentic Christian faith is always one generation from extinction. Each new generation must decide for itself whether to affirm or repudiate Christian teaching. What often makes the difference is the degree of integrity and authenticity the prior generation displays. My father's integrity and honest convictions could not be casually ignored. His deep love for me I could measure by his willingness to proscribe and to discipline. I could not honestly use the "rules" to "jump ship"; I would have to assume that responsibility for myself.

No more dreaded form of punishment exists than a

man-to-man talk with a father who knows God. It is no picnic to hear what the Bible has to say about a rebellious spirit and wayward conduct. Nor is it very comfortable to listen to a prayer offered to God on your behalf. In the end, however, it may accomplish more than raising welts on bare legs. Perhaps the answer lies in the judicious use of both.

Later, my father's integrity prevailed in my struggle to compromise God's call to preach. If I could have found a way to negate the authenticity of my father's faith and life, it would have provided the needed escape hatch. Some thirty years later, returning to Tucson as district superintendent, I discovered that my childhood friends with permissive parents were seldom active in any church. Those who had "suffered through with me" were often pillars in some church.

Parsonage Life

Family life in a Methodist parsonage often violated fundamental needs for privacy and personal tastes. The parsonage was normally adjacent to the church as a convenience for strangers and parishioners. As community property, parishioners regarded it as a facility readily available for church use at any time of the day or night. Thus, a living room might be needed for a Sunday school class, a kitchen could be put to use to serve a church dinner, or a bathroom turned into a public rest room. To make matters worse in an age when doors were seldom locked, some visitors maintained the attitude that one should not need to knock in order to gain entrance. The highly regarded principle that "a minister isn't in it for the money" lent reinforcement to such practices. They equated the call of God with poverty and overwork. Unfortunately, many church members readily and willingly saw to it that such principles remained in force.

The minister's wife in such a case was expected to accept without complaint a home furnished with whatever castoffs parishioners might be willing to donate to the cause. Perhaps church members felt that no materialistic desires should tarnish the pristine purity of the ecclesiastical diadem. The typical parsonage was a situation quite out of keeping with Ethel McPheeter's affluent home background, but she did adjust.

In retrospect, one must remember that meager living was commonplace in those days and, until more recent times, considered a virtue. A person with self-reliance "made do" with available resources. Poverty was no badge of shame and one's sense of self-respect rejected any thought of public welfare.

People took pride in their work; their word was their bond. As a result, one could be poor without feeling victimized.

When it came to church finance, the congregation expected their pastor to lead the way. A tithe was used as the plumb line for giving since it was a concept clearly delineated in the Scriptures. JC never wavered in his practice of "storehouse tithing." He never permitted illness and a mounting burden of debt to compromise this practice. God's money was a sacred trust and "came off the top." His conviction made giving a joy rather than a burden.

The McPheeters' family budget seldom could provide much beyond basic necessities. No new bicycles appeared under the Christmas tree. The food was wholesome and adequate, even though fried mush appeared frequently on the menu. The family wardrobe was marginal and utilitarian, with one suitable outfit for Sunday use, and Easter was never a fashion parade. A new garment for a growing child, especially a boy, usually came a size too large and would be worn until a size too small.

The minister's wife wore her good Sunday dress like a never-changing uniform. The one time the McPheeters became the recipients of a "missionary barrel" was in Montana. Whatever high hopes the family might have entertained quickly dissipated as it disgorged unusable gleanings out of the Victorian Era.

Family memories are still vivid of the time generous parishioners decided to take Ethel shopping and let her select a complete ensemble without any regard for cost. What an exhilarating and happy experience, the first of its kind since her marriage, to return home with a complete outfit in the latest style. She chose a suit of brown velveteen with blouse, shoes, hat and purse to match. Of course, such a thing could not go unnoticed, and some criticized what they took to be extravagance by the parsonage family. Even this could not obscure the happiness this very thoughtful gift brought to Ethel's Tucson experience.

JC's sermon preparation and the colossal demands of a growing parish seldom provided much time for family recreation unless, of course, it was somehow related to church life: a Sunday school picnic, a class outing, a church softball league, a Boy Scout overnight, vacation Bible school activities, or family camp. When annual conference met in Northern Arizona, it often included the bonus of a three-day fishing excursion to Mormon Lake or an overnight visit to the Grand Canyon.

Hunting merited a different set of priorities. The desert teemed with rabbit, quail, dove and white wing. JC found it especially easy to bag a limit of dove or white wing and return home in time for breakfast. What a memorable Christmas it was when, as a boy of ten, I received a coveted .410 shotgun and graduated from spectator to participant in the hunt.

One of our desert hunts nearly ended in tragedy. As a dutiful twelve-year-old, I was walking behind my father when I saw that he was about to step on a rattlesnake. My cry of danger caused him to leap for safety, but in the wrong direction. Although a quick shot killed the snake and the cushion of sand spared JC any broken bones, badly torn ligaments in each knee made the trip home a journey of intense pain for him. A high fever wracked his body for several days. Indeed, it would be many years before he overcame the lingering effects of this experience.

Distance, money, and time mitigated against many visits back to the old homestead in Missouri. Visiting Grandmother Chilton was always a memorable experience, though. Her garden produced a cornucopia of food: the storm cellar overflowed with homecanned fruit and vegetables, hams hung suspended in the smokehouse, and the kitchen was filled daily with the aroma of freshly baked bread and pies. There was butter to be churned, blackberries and gooseberries to pluck, chickens to feed, eggs to gather, a cow to be milked and pigs to be "slopped." Lilacs grew in her front yard, and her old-fashioned porch swing became a center for conversation. There were family sings around the piano and tall tales about pioneer days. For grandchildren it was a fleeting trip into paradise.

One trip to Missouri had to be cancelled on short notice due to my mother's emergency appendectomy. An ill mother was a domestic disaster for the McPheeters family. Father in the kitchen was a culinary catastrophe. He could do two things: boil eggs and make potato soup. By the time a simple meal was over, the kitchen would look as if it had been sacked.

One bright side emerged, however, when he decided to help alleviate my crushing disappointment by granting me permission to walk to town and attend the Saturday morning cowboy movies, with their nickel popcorn and their chilling serial episodes of adventure. Up to that time most entertainment had been confined to school plays, church choir musicals and the week-long events of summer chautauqua. Only twice had I been to the movies, but "The Thief of Baghdad" and "Ben Hur" had been enough to whet a boy's appetite for more.

And thou shalt be called, the repairer of the breach, the restorer of paths to dwell in.

(Isaiah 58:12b, KJV)

4

The San Francisco Years

"California, Here We Come"

Somehow during this maze of activity JC found time to write his first book. *Sons of God* was a volume of sermons on Christian discipleship. Gordon Gordon served as market manager with mail order shipments going out from the parsonage. The first edition sold out within a few months.

Sons of God was a volume destined to be a landmark, the seedbed for JC's ever-widening ministry through the printed word. It would also play a key role in his next appointment, for it brought him to the attention of Mrs. Lizzie H. Glide.

Mrs. Glide was in the process of fulfilling her dream for buiding an evangelistic center in the heart of downtown San Francisco. She had high hopes of luring "Fighting Bob" Shuler out of Los Angeles to lead the new project. Despite the proffered gift of his own radio station and other inducements, Shuler declined to move. He did, however, suggest the name of J. C. McPheeters as an alternative. After reading *Sons of God*, Mrs. Glide was fully convinced that here was the man needed to turn her dreams into reality.

In the meantime, Henry Clay Morrison, then president of Asbury College, had become aware of JC's evangelical fervor and solid achievements. Morrison had held two revival meetings

59

in University Church, and spent a memorable day with JC on the desert hunting quail. Morrison's conviction grew that McPheeters was the person needed to become his successor. The initial step was to nominate him for a place on the Asbury College Board. Later JC was given a page in *The Herald* for a weekly article.

JC's itch to write was further satisfied with the publication of *Sunshine and Victory*, the saga of his victorious battle over tuberculosis and the inspirational stories of others who had coped with illnesses and triumphed over them. It was a ray of hope for those living under the shadow of death.

In 1930 America stood on the threshold of momentous change. The economic scars of the trauma of The Great Depression seemed to encourage the accelerating shift from a rural to an urban society and wholesale modification of free enterprise by increasing social controls. The nation was shifting from a posture of isolation to military power and world leadership. JC, caught up in this movement of change, would find himself in radically new fields of service and opportunity.

At this same time, the Western Area of the Methodist Church, South, was about to receive a more vital kind of leadership. Arthur J. Moore was elected bishop in 1930, leaving the pulpit of First Church in Birmingham, Alabama, to become the youngest person in the episcopal office. In keeping with time-honored custom, he was duly appointed to the Western Area. Moore arrived on the scene just in time to become deeply involved with the final stages of Mrs. Glide's dream.

Located in the heart of San Francisco's tenderloin area, the building complex was well under way by the time Bishop Moore arrived. The sanctuary had been located on the second floor, at an added cost of $25,000, to make room for ground-floor shop rentals and a walk-in evangelistic hall. An adjacent six-story apartment, with a street-level restaurant, provided housing for the ministerial staff, along with small apartments and single rooms for working people. The bishop's pressing task was to find and appoint the right man to lead Glide Memorial Church.

Julian C. McPheeters was the man selected for the job. Bishop Moore's invitation to move to San Francisco was a complete surprise. Although intrigued by the opportunity, JC needed answers to two basic questions. Would the climate in the Bay Area be adverse to his health? And how would apartment life in the heart of a big city affect our family life? San Francisco was rated the number one "sin city" in America. Two thirds of the population had no church affiliation, only four percent were Protestant. Law enforcement was so lax that speakeasies flourished and gambling was openly available while pimps and prostitutes walked the streets with impunity. Would it be fair to bring two teen-agers into an environment so filled with paganism, hedonism and materialism?

In the end, JC's reply to the Bishop was affirmative. He would increase his insurance and move to San Francisco. The McPheeters family arrived in this city of destiny in early November, 1930.

The Story of Lizzie Glide

Mrs. Glide's story reads like a chronicle out of the pages of the Bible. Born Lizzie Helen Snyder, October 1, 1852, in Bossier Parish, Louisiana, she was the third of ten children. Her physician father, Dr. Thornton Snyder, was a devout man, so it was not surprising that she "gave her heart to Jesus" at a tender age.

In 1867, for reasons not clear, Dr. Snyder went to California and settled in Sacramento. Two years later his family joined him. Their plans to join the local Presbyterian Church were abandoned because of the unsympathetic and abusive attitudes toward Southerners. As a consequence, the family united with the Southern Methodist Church. Here Lizzie taught Sunday school and eventually met Joseph Glide.

Joseph Henry Glide was born near Taunton, England, August 15, 1835. At seventeen he sailed for Philadelphia. City life proved to be unsatisfactory. Glide longed for an environment where he could use the expertise and knowledge of cattle he had acquired under his father's tutelage. In 1854, he made his way to Grass Valley, California, at the very peak of the gold rush mania.

Wisely, Glide resisted the temptation to search for gold. Men had to eat, and he would supply that need. In time, he became one of the leading stockmen of the state, acquiring vast holdings in Sacramento, Solano, Yolo, Colusa, Glenn, Tulare and Kern Counties.

He married Lizzie Snyder on December 7, 1871. The union was blessed with two sons and three daughters. Their continuing prosperity seemed symbolized in their Sacramento mansion, a showplace, reflecting gracious living and political influence.

In February, 1889, the celebrated evangelist Sam P. Jones visited Sacramento for a revival meeting. His message challenged God's people to live lives of complete consecration. This "second work of grace" has had a variety of designations in theological circles: sanctification, perfect love, holiness of heart and life, the second blessing, the gift of the Spirit. In lay terms it simply meant unconditional discipleship, a concept clearly enunciated by Jesus.

Lizzie Glide, profoundly touched by Jones' challenge, desired to respond affirmatively. But, as an obedient wife in a patriarchal society, she first consulted her husband. Would he be offended or oppose this commitment on her part? After a full and lengthy discussion of the matter, and receiving no objections, Lizzie knelt alone in her room and consecrated her life wholly to God. The following day she made public this private act of surrender.

From this point on her life had new meaning and direction. Bible study classes and prayer bands turned the Glide mansion into a great soul-saving way station. She shocked and scandalized her peers by appearing on street corners to give her testimony. She was the moving force behind the establishment of an Inner City Mission. Lizzie visited the sick, the dying and those in jail. She responded to the cries of the lonely, the unloved and the unlovely. Her effectiveness for the cause of Christ became so evident that her husband once confided to a friend: "I believe my wife is leading more souls to Christ than all the ministers in the city."

As she shared herself, she also gave her wealth. "You can give without loving, but you can't love without giving!" As Jesus said, "A good tree beareth good fruit." The Great Commission took on a new depth of meaning and urgency for her. She saw that much needed doing that required money. In common with the wives of that day, however, Mrs. Glide had no money or property of her own. She depended on the generosity of her husband, and economizing on household expenses was woefully inadequate. Consequently, she adopted a new strategy. From then on she requested monetary gifts for Christmas, birthdays and anniversary occasions in lieu of other costly remembrances. It was a move that greatly enhanced her "war chest for God."

Lizzie was her husband's designated heir when he died in 1906. Suddenly, with little or no experience in the business world, she found herself shouldering large responsibilities for a financial empire. But with God as her partner and prayer as a source of wisdom, she learned quickly and well. Bankers and captains of industry soon discovered she had one of the keenest business minds in the state.

Rather than have her children waiting around, perhaps

impatiently, for their mother to die, the day came when she called them together and announced her decision to divide the estate in six equal parts. Moreover, in a scene reminiscent of Abraham and Lot, she informed them that they would be given first choice in the selection of property. After the division, Mrs. Glide had among her assets certain "worthless" acres near Bakersfield, shunned by her children.

Some years later oil was discovered under this "worthless" land and Mrs. Glide gained a bountiful resource for her Christian philanthropy. Her largess encompassed the globe: missionary support, student scholarships, college dormitories for girls, low-cost housing for working women, a radio station for Christian broadcasting, church extension funds for Third World nations.

As the years passed she found herself living at the edge of a mission field as great as any in the world. Frequent visits to San Francisco gave her a vision for a great center for evangelism and Christian nurture to be located at the city's very center. Its primary mission would be to proclaim Christ's Gospel of "free salvation for all men and full salvation from all sin." Realizing that dream became the culmination of a lifetime of giving.

Glide Memorial Church

Life in a great port city with its cosmopolitan tastes, high incidence of transiency and apartment house living has a heartbeat all its own. It becomes a way-station for singles, a playground for pleasure seekers, a conduit for business and culture, a dumping ground for poverty, a sanctuary of anonymity for the lawless, a land of promise for the talented and the innovative. Cities affect the fabric of society in definitive ways, whether as magnets of hope or islands of despair. Cities either strengthen or weaken a nation. "As the city goes, so goes the nation!"

For the church to abandon the city is to betray her mission to be "salt" and "leaven" within the social order. Glide Church was established as a bold and innovative response to this challenge. In San Francisco the task would not be easy. Factors of space and climate encouraged families with young children to live outside the city. Noise, traffic and wall-to-wall pavement substituted for lawns, trees and grass. Persons on the way up in the life of corporate America would pause here only briefly. Those who would build a church in inner San Francisco would have to face the prospect of "making brick without straw."

JC reported for duty about three months prior to the completion of the new Glide facilities. In the interim, the Fitzgerald Memorial Church on Bush Street served as his headquarters and provided temporary living quarters. Started in 1853, this musty edifice was Southern Methodism's only beachhead in the city. Though it had been served by able pastors, two of whom eventually served with distinction as bishops, the church had never prospered. In 1930, Fitzgerald Memorial was all but comatose, capable of supplying only seventy names for the initial membership of Glide Church.

Under these circumstances, the new pastor could not have been faulted had he used this interval to mark time to become better oriented to the situation. But JC plunged in with his usual vigor and enthusiasm, proclaiming without apology the redemptive love of a risen Christ. When the time came to move, he brought with him a growing congregation of dedicated people.

The Methodist denomination took great pride in this new venture and gave it national publicity. An extensive article complete with pictures appeared in July 1931 in *The Missionary Voice*. It was captioned "An Adventure in Home Missions." The author called it "one of the most unique and bold attempts to solve a problem in home missions," namely, reaching the heart of a great city for Christ. Some who hoped that what the Apostle Paul did for Ephesus might now be repeated through this new evangelical thrust.

The church sanctuary opened its doors for worship on January 11, 1931. Two weeks later the Glide apartments were ready for occupancy. Bishop Moore became the first episcopal leader to live in the West when he moved with his family into a sixth-floor apartment. The bishop's residency was a tribute to Mrs. Glide's generosity and lifted morale throughout the conference area, even though it terminated in less than two years. The McPheeters family occupied a similar apartment on the fifth floor.

At this period of time, the economy of the nation was in shambles. Men stood on street corners selling apples for a living. Unemployment was rampant and those fortunate to have a job might work a full week for eighteen dollars. One could get a steak dinner for as little as thirty cents. Cafeterias advertised "all you can eat for fifty cents" with chamber music during the dinner hour as an added bonus. Some rooms in a first class hotel could be had for two dollars and fifty cents a night. All in all it was not a very promising economic environment in which to launch a new church. Indeed, in order not to frighten people away, the church ad proclaimed, "A Church Free of Debt."

Again, the central emphasis of the Glide Memorial ministry was a vigorous proclamation of the Gospel. Around this would cluster, as the program unfolded, a group of supporting activities to nurture, strengthen and demonstrate the relevance and power of God at individual and corporate levels.

The first Friday of each month was set aside as a day of prayer and fasting. A prayer room was open twenty-four hours a day. JC organized and established a Tither's League and an annual School of Christian Workers. Revival meetings provided city exposure to such nationally known leaders as Henry Clay Morrison, Bishop Arthur J. Moore, John Brown, Bob Shuler and William H. Evans. A Fisherman's Club provided the outreach needed for follow-up calls and membership cultivation.

Radio became a regular adjunct for meeting special needs: "Fellowship of the Air," "Shut-in-Circle," "Pocket Testament League of the Air," "Religion and Social Issues." In 1937 when attempts were made to quash "The Atherton Investigation" into civic corruption in high places, JC used the radio to sound the alarm and maintain public pressure to prevent a whitewash. Newspapers carried the full text of his messages. He was called to City Hall for conferences with the mayor and other civic leaders. Despite telephone threats on his life, the campaign continued until indictments and prison terms were handed down.

JC edited a weekly column in the San Francisco Examiner for many years, "Religion In The News." He added a prison pastor to the staff for work at San Quentin and the county jail. Another member of the staff worked with juvenile delinquents.

To help foster spiritual growth and development, JC had a devotional booklet, *Today with God,* printed monthly. It offered a systematic coverage of the Bible, book by book, over a two-year period. Each day featured suggested Bible readings, a golden text for the day, a brief exegesis and a closing prayer. Later, Grover Emmons, a ministerial colleague named to be the first editor of *The Upper Room,* came to examine and evaluate this booklet as part of a study to select a format for the new publication. Some years later, Bishop William C. Martin introduced Dr. McPheeters to a national convocation as "the spiritual father" of *The Upper Room.*

To help bring the members of a scattered parish together, serve the needs of lonely people and provide a low-cost dinner for those unable to enjoy the benefits of home cooking, the church featured a fellowship dinner on Wednesday evenings. For many this function served as an introduction into the larger dimensions of church life. It also encouraged attendance at the prayer meeting that followed.

Unemployment and poverty were a constant source of concern. On Thursday nights the church provided a free meal for indigents. A voucher system was worked out to provide lodging at The Salvation Army and The Volunteers of America. Meal tickets, good at nearby restaurants, guaranteed that no person need go away hungry. Unfortunately, a high percentage seeking help wanted only money for alcohol or gambling and would litter the premises with discarded tickets and vouchers.

The church made every effort to help people find employment, even odd jobs and temporary work. Evidence of JC's deep personal concern was expressed with unadorned simplicity when I discussed with him the prospect of my taking a part-time job as a stockroom clerk in a local department store. After a time of listening he suggested that it might be better, since our family was not in dire need, for me to leave the job open for someone whose circumstances were less favorable. His wish was respected even though, at the time, JC's principle seemed unlikely to make any real impact on the Great Depression.

JC became a pioneer in the use of motion pictures as valid tools for the church. The phenomenal success of the movie "The Grapes of Wrath" in sensitizing the conscience of America to the plight of migratory workers offered convincing proof. What better way to highlight social problems and deal with biblical truths? The time came when JC regularly used films at the Sunday evening service.

It was not enough for JC to join the chorus of protest against the conditions of migrant life. He went into the fields to see for himself. The results were two sixteen-millimeter films showing positive ways of overcoming this blight. One was called "The Trail of the Migrants" and the other "Grapes of Gladness." Since the general public seems more attracted to bad news tragedies than to good news triumphs, the themes lacked commercial interest. However, they were used extensively by church groups throughout the state of California. This success encouraged JC to develop other films on a variety of themes.

Adequate exercise was a nagging problem for McPheeters as pastor of this demanding church. JC found that the most practical means of exercise for him was to walk the hills of San Francisco while he memorized Scripture. Later he would discover the trout streams of Santa Cruz County and the duck blinds of the wet lands north of Sacramento. He even learned the art of deep-sea fishing. But most of these activities were all too seldom enjoyed due to the limitations of time.

Ultimately JC would discover something else that would fill his need for regular exercise and become a permanent part of a life-long and growing habit. It all stemmed from my desire to become another Charles Atlas by answering an ad for a set of hand dumbbells. The routine proved to be too dull and tedious for me, and I looked for more interesting ways to build up muscle. JC, though, was glad to claim the dumbbells as his own, and he adopted an exercise routine. Those same dumbbells remained in constant use well into JC's tenth decade.

If there were times when the task of building a church and expanding its outreach seemed like plowing the waves, JC gave no outward evidence of it. When he trained young leaders only to see them transferred, he took comfort in knowing they would take root somewhere else. Transciency might put limits on membership figures, but it did offer vast opportunities for influencing multitudes of people. Even so, at the end of eighteen years of service JC left behind the largest church in the conference, whose rolls contained five percent of the Protestant church membership in San Francisco. Some 3,600 members had joined Glide Memorial Church, almost sixty per cent on profession of faith.

The Little-Known Story of the Glide Foundation

At the time that Mrs. Lizzie Glide made her decision to move ahead with her dream of an evangelistic center in the heart of San Francisco, she established the Glide Foundation. The Foundation's Deed and Declaration of Trust stated that: "All preaching and teaching in connection with the work of the foundation shall set forth the doctrine of the Deity of Jesus Christ, His atoning sufferings and death for the whole human race, His bodily resurrection from the dead, His ascension, and the work of the Holy Spirit in teaching, convincing, and witnessing to the pardoning power and sanctifying influences and powers; and that nothing shall ever be preached that shall controvert any of the said doctrines." Julian C. McPheeters faithfully fulfilled the mandate of this mission for the eighteen years that he pastored Glide Church. How that trust was later abrogated is a story for a later chapter.

On the surface it seems paradoxical that Lizzie Glide failed to provide any substantial funds for the work of the foundation. As a matter of fact, the principle was quite in keeping with her past charitable largess. She understood the perils of easy money and the waste and dependency it so often encouraged. Where capital gifts were involved, such as a college dormitory for girls or a low-cost apartment house for working women, the projects were designed to generate the income needed to meet maintenance and operational costs.

The real financial strength of the Glide Foundation came only with the acquisition of the Californian Hotel. The story of how this came about is an amazing feat attributable mainly to the business acumen, personal integrity and persuasive powers of J. C. McPheeters.

The year was 1935, and the nation was still in the harsh and paralyzing grip of the Great Depression. The Californian Hotel was a seventeen-story, three hundred-room facility, one block north of Glide Church. A contractor had built it as a personal investment just prior to the collapse of the stock market in 1929. Eventually the bank holding the mortgage had to foreclose. When JC learned that the bank, anxious to get out of the real estate business, had it on the market for immediate sale, he hastened to investigate.

Such a move on his part took both faith and nerve, especially since five merged congregations of the Methodist Episcopal Church, North, had built the William Taylor Hotel, incorporating their worship facilities in it. Their experiment had turned out to be a financial disaster and they, too, were in the process of losing their property. What made another churchman think the hard-headed business community would welcome overtures from any ecclesiastical organization? Undismayed, JC made an appointment to see Parker Maddox. Yes, the property was on the block for $750,000, just one-third the original cost of construction.

JC sought time to meet with Glide Foundation Board of Trustees and seek their approval. He proposed the following counteroffer to the bank: purchase price, $700,000; nothing down; monthly payments to be made out of operating income; present hotel manager to be retained; no encumbrances of any kind on any other Glide Foundation assets.

The immediate reaction of the foundation's board was opposition. No one can know how much was generated by distaste for operating a hotel and how much was due to the incredulity of the proposed counteroffer. Judge Waiste, then a member of the Supreme Court of California, and Mrs. Glide herself vigorously asserted no businessman would take seriously the terms outlined by JC. After much debate a consensus was reached to let the proposal be made. They had nothing to lose since, obviously, nothing would come of it.

To the amazement of all, Maddox agreed to the contractural terms and the foundation found itself, thirty days later, in the hotel business. It seems certain that for the banker involved, J. C. McPheeters was the foundation. Approval of the offer was a vote of confidence in JC's integrity and business acumen.

The first thing the foundation did was to close the bar, in keeping with JC's temperance principles. The hotel community and the alcoholic beverage industry were scandalized and angry over this action. They held the common belief that "no first class hotel in San Francisco can operate without a bar." Just to make certain, they established a boycott which terminated all referrals to the hotel by other local hotels and eliminated the reciprocal advertising folders so common in the hotel lobbies of that day.

Such an economic threat could not be brushed aside. JC's response was to contact churches across the state and the constituency of the California Temperance Federation announcing the availability of a "temperance hotel" in San Francisco. Within the month the hotel had an occupancy rate well ahead of any of its rivals. So far as anyone knows, only one guest moved out because the bar was closed.

A companion problem involved the coffee shop at the corner of the building. It had several years to run on a lease that merely stipulated "nothing be served in violation of the law." The repeal of the eighteenth amendment had opened the door for the dispensing of beer. The hotel management worked out a financial subsidy so that beer would not be served. Even opponents came to respect this kind of integrity.

Cooperation Without Compromise

Seeing the good and accenting the positive were hallmarks of Julian C. McPheeters' life. In October, 1950, he wrote in a letter to his close friend Dr. Robert "Fighting Bob" Shuler, "I had rather err on the side of charity than intolerance." Jesus' prayer for the unity of His people was something he honored and affirmed. JC believed that a divisive spirit, especially over secondary issues, greatly hampered and denied the Church's mission in the world. He was equally at home serving as president of the California Temperance Federation and presiding as president of the San Francisco Council of Churches. He was, as a matter of fact, one of the founders of The Northern California Council of Churches.

Pardon Me, Sir

On the eve of his departure from San Francisco, JC received a letter, dated May 10, 1948, from Dr. Hughbert H. Landram, Executive Director of the San Francisco Council of Churches, who wrote: "It is hard to think of your not being with us in person after next month! We will miss you, both personally, and for your ecumenical spirit, which I give major credit for our Protestant forces not being split in San Francisco!"

This guiding principle of "cooperation without compromise" enabled him to avoid the perils of demanding primary loyalty to secondary issues. He understood the true meaning of the "protestant principle" to be one of "affirmation," rather than mere "negative protest." "Pro-testare," from which the term protestant was derived, means "testimony-for." JC held Christian unity to be more a matter of "spirit" than of "structure."

He was, like John Wesley, an eager advocate of church renewal. He wanted to recover and maintain for Methodism the vitality of her spiritual heritage. Yet he understood from the historic perspective that authentic church reform is a "pushed out" rather than a "come out" movement: Jesus was repudiated by temple authorities; Luther was excommunicated by his church; Wesley was denied the right to preach in Anglican pulpits. Criticism without viable alternatives he saw as easy; anyone can abandon ship.

The record shows that JC could apply this principle of "augmentation" without any rupture on his part of a spirit of unity and unbroken fellowship. The formation of a Bay Area Evangelical Ministerial Alliance was a case in point. It was organized to sponsor an annual lectureship that featured distinguished evangelical scholars who were consistently ignored by more liberal forums. Careful to avoid any conflict in dates with its member churches, this group enriched the intellectual and spiritual life of the Bay Area by providing a platform for such scholars as Edwin Lewis, Charles Erdman, Andrew Blackwood and John McKay.

A similar evidence of this approach manifested itself when the conference summer camp program abandoned evangelical concerns, refusing even to allocate a single camp for these purposes. A group of concerned individuals and churches then banded together to keep this tradition alive. They rented facilities at Mount Hermon and held their first camp in 1939. The following year JC was elected president and became a compelling factor in the camp's future and growth.

San Francisco Years

The story of the Redwood Christian Park is one more illustration of how "God moves in mysterious ways His wonders to perform." Growth dictated the need to purchase a site for camp development. When 200 acres of magnificent redwoods became available in 1943, a concerned layman rushed from Oakland to Boulder Creek to sign a sales agreement and submit a personal check for the earnest money. The asking price was $24,000.

Site development began with advice from the forestry service as to which trees to harvest for the good of future growth. The sale of lumber more than covered the purchase price of the property and provided materials for a large, all-purpose dining hall, kitchen and meeting rooms. Within a few years a hodge-podge of tents and campers gave way to a complex of modern buildings capable of sleeping five hundred people.

Elements in the conference became more and more critical as they perceived the camp's growing influence. Something in the bureaucratic mind gets nervous and agitated when the Holy Spirit works outside the bounds of institutional programs. Eventually, the conference decided to send one of its conference program directors to experience first-hand what was going on. Before the week ended this executive's wife was gloriously converted. The risk factor of such an investigation was evidently too high, for the conference never repeated it again. The passing years, thankfully, have seen the end of most overt criticism, and the program has become generally well regarded.

Today the Redwood Christian Park operates year-round and provides facilities for many different groups. Serviced by a competent resident staff, as many as 13,000 people use it in a given year. Two family camps, with special camps for children, high school and college youth, train laymen and send forth a steady stream of ministerial and missionary candidates for the United Methodist Church. Perhaps these fruits are what make some critics most nervous.

Those who "march to a different drummer" are often suspect and so are seldom honored with policy-making roles. Even so, JC was twice asked to serve as a district superintendent, and each time he asked to be excused. He was a member of the Uniting Conference of Methodism in 1939, served on the general conference board of evangelism, was president of both jurisdictional and conference boards of evangelism, was president of his annual conference Board of Church Extension, and was a member of the 1947 Ecumenical Conference of World Methodism.

71

However, he did not hesitate to play an active role in organizations beyond the range of United Methodist endorsement. He was on the boards of both The National Association of Evangelicals and The National Holiness Association. He was a frequent speaker at various camp meeting associations across the nation. He joined Ford Philpot in his African evangelistic crusade. He at times served as national president of The Deeper Life Conference and espoused the cause of faith missionary societies as needed adjuncts to mainline denominational ministries.

The vaunted pluralism of United Methodism has at times denied its own tenets by the selective policies sometimes employed to keep evangelicals from a role in the church in keeping with their grassroots numerical strength. JC, though, did not allow his perception of such practices to distort his life by any harvest of bitterness, disappointment or envy. Love for his church remained as steadfast as his love for his Lord. It was enough to be in the center of God's will and to know when to hold on and when to let go.

Such a spirit made him a living legend. When JC spoke on the floor of his annual conference, he was often greeted with a standing ovation. One of the finest tributes ever given him was made by a ministerial colleague of mine who has impeccable liberal credentials: "If everyone in the holiness movement had your father's spirit I would change my theology today." I did appreciate this compliment, but it raises a further question: Why be the last to do the Truth? Why not be a pioneer and lead the way? JC was such a pioneer!

The Flying Pig

When JC and a friend were driving to a meeting in Modesto one morning, it seemed like just another routine trip. The highway, the most heavily traveled one in the state, was the primary artery between San Francisco and Los Angeles. Nothing seemed out of the ordinary until the sudden appearance of a flying pig.

This incongruous vision of a pig in midair triggered JC's vigorous application of the brakes combined with a variety of evasive turns of the steering wheel. As the car lurched to a stop, JC could see the truck from which the pig had catapulted disappearing down the highway, well beyond the summons of any horn blast on his part.

It was idle to speculate on how this one animal had managed to wriggle free from the top compartment of a farm-to-market truck and launch out into space. The important thing now, especially for JC who had grown up on a farm, was to save a stricken animal from possible suffering and a lingering death. Cursory examination, however, revealed the animal had only been stunned by the ordeal. The most humane and sensible thing seemed to be to put the pig in the back of the car, be on time for the appointment, and then hope to find a way to make contact with the owner.

With the business of the day taken care of, the problem of the pig moved to the top of the agenda. First, JC asked the sheriff to help in trying to locate the legal owner. After several futile phone calls the next logical step seemed to be a visit to the local slaughterhouse. But this tactic proved futile for lack of a certificate of legal ownership that would empower JC with the right to dispose of a pig in this way.

This dead-end alley did trigger an inspiration. Why not sell the animal to some farmer and donate the proceeds to the cause of missions? Surely on his way home he could find a farmer who would be glad to acquire the pig. Stops along the way soon established that only a pig farmer wanted anything to do with pigs. And not a pig farmer was to be found.

Arriving home with a fully recovered pig peering out the back window of the car made finding a temporary haven for this new guest most urgent. Ethel, somewhat indignant, vetoed any use of her kitchen for such a purpose. One hope might be an appeal to a parishioner who operated a chicken farm across the Bay. With an amused chuckle this man agreed to provide emergency housing if someone could deliver the animal.

In the end, JC took on this chauffering chore and somehow convinced his wife to go with him for the drive. It turned out to be a trip that invited stares of amazement and amusement. It also carried with it the aroma of a pig sty. However, this reprieve enabled JC to leave for an upcoming conference in Salt Lake City with a clear conscience.

About this time the district superintendent asked if Glide Church could help cover a shortfall in the project to establish Methodism's first black church in San Francisco. The church had already given a fair share quota of $2,000, but "Would the D.S. be willing to settle for a missionary pig?" JC inquired.

Thus originated a plan for a dinner benefit whose centerpiece on the menu would feature a pig that had dared to fly. JC agreed to have the animal fattened, slaughtered and cooked. The district superintendent asked district churches to sell tickets at $10 each, a handsome sum at that time. The project generated a fund of amusement and expanded awareness of an important home missions project. The end result was a profit in excess of the funds needed. Not bad for the chance encounter with one ordinary pig.

The Glide Christian Service Center

Hundreds of thousands of military personnel funneled through the great port of San Francisco during World War II. They wandered the streets of the crowded metropolis bearing the burdens of fear, the pain of loneliness, the agony of faded dreams, and the traumas inflicted by war's nightmare of hell. A variety of splendid efforts helped grapple with this problem, yet needs far outstripped available resources.

Thus, in the fall of 1943, as the war in the Pacific gathered momentum, the Glide Christian Service Center opened its doors. I had deferred my own entrance into the military chaplaincy to return to San Francisco in order to participate in this remarkable enterprise. Despite wartime shortages, helpful friends had somehow found carpeting and furnishings needed for a spacious and attractive facility at street level. It was designed to be "a home away from home," an informal center of hospitality with an underlying spiritual ministry. The center, staffed by volunteers, many of them motherly types, were trained to listen and to deal compassionately with problems. We kept a snack bar stocked with homemade goodies, soft drinks, tea and coffee, and made available quiet places for reading, writing and listening to music. The Christian Service Center became "a place apart" where thousands would feel the warmth of Christian love and gain strengthened faith for the perils and hardships of an unknown future.

JC encouraged church families to open their homes to those in uniform. He had a hand in scheduling parties and special events to help relieve loneliness and boredom and to enlarge avenues for friendship. As a result of the church's friendliness, several hundred in the Armed Services attended church on an average Sunday. Many renewed or made an initial surrender to God. Some of these eventually became ministers or missionaries.

One of the most distinguished of these converts was Edmund W. Robb, who has gone on to become a distinguished United Methodist pastor, noted evangelist and influential leader of evangelical causes. He has written, "The real influence in bringing me to Christ was the ministry of Dr. McPheeters—he inspires enthusiasm and a desire to serve the Lord." Ed Robb tells that the night he knelt at the altar of Glide Church and surrendered his life to Christ, he left with a friend, threw a half-used pack of cigarettes as far across the street as he could and announced to his companion, "I'm going to preach!"

Another alumnus of this group, Richard A. Gifford, wrote in 1974, "Your mark on my life remains: your warmth of Christian love when I lived at the Glide apartments; your understanding when I came home from the Marines in World War II, injured, confused and discouraged; your generosity in making a Glide scholarship available to me so I could go to Asbury. This watering of the seed and cultivating of the plant continues to bear fruit in souls because of God's working through my ministry."

J. C. McPheeters, age twelve, with his
mother and two sisters

JC and Ethel, April 16, 1944
in San Francisco

H. C. Morrison and JC on Asbury
College Campus, mid 1930s

JC and W. D. Turkington laying the
cornerstone of Estes Chapel in 1952

E. Stanley Jones and JC,
1960s

Alexander Reid, E. A. Seamands,
and J. C. McPheeters

JC pulling 400 pounds

JC with Sherman Thomas

JC receiving "Man of God" award, 1982

President David McKenna greets JC at his 52nd Asbury Commencement

JC in The Glide Memorial Church
pulpit, 1940s

Always be prepared to make a defense to any one who calls you to account for the hope that is in you, yet do it with gentleness and reverence.

(I Peter 3:15, RSV)

5

Mr. President: Asbury Theological Seminary

Shoehorned Into the Job

When Henry Clay Morrison died in the spring of 1942, his mantle fell on the shoulders of Julian C. McPheeters. This was the culmination of a twenty-year grooming process that began when Morrison nominated him for membership on the Asbury Board of Trustees, the governing body for both college and seminary. Eventually he was elected chairman of the board. A later phase found him functioning as associate editor of *The Herald* and writing a weekly page in the publication. Finally, Morrison wrested a promise from McPheeters that he would become editor of *The Herald* upon Morrison's death.

On June 5, 1936, Morrison wrote, "After much consultation with wife, with reference as to who shall become editor of *The Herald* in case of my death, we have decided that you are the man, and have specified same in our will. I am writing this note to urge you to accept this position and I feel sure you can do the work so efficiently that *The Herald* shall not suffer on my death, but go forward for even better things."

Morrison's death left a tremendous void to be filled. The

situation was made still more acute by the immediate need to locate the seminary on its own campus with a board of trustees separate from Asbury College. This was a mandatory requirement for the accreditation of both the seminary and the college. Therefore, the office of seminary president had to be filled without delay.

JC was offered the office of president of the developing seminary almost immediately. It was an offer that he at first summarily rejected. However, persuasive voices pressed him to accept the office on a temporary basis so the search committee could have time to secure a permanent replacement. McPheeters' reluctant consent was given, provided no member of the official board of his church objected. Thus was the second president of Asbury Theological Seminary shoehorned, at least temporarily, into the job.

Asbury Theological Seminary had very little to offer its new president: one all-purpose building, a faculty of five, a student body of sixty, an annual budget of $15,000, no endowment, and no assured income. At this time, a global war for freedom's survival placed heavy demands on a nation's manpower and resources. When the search committee failed to find a candidate for president who was both suitable and willing, the committee returned to McPheeters with the message that unless he continued on the school would have to be closed. The reality of such a dire threat left JC with no alternative. It was thus the mandate of this crisis that compelled the "temporary" to become fixed in concrete.

For a man of lesser faith and ability the odds would have seemed hopeless. So many crucial things were needed at once: money for increased faculty, land for more buildings, housing for married students, books for an enlarged library, ways to meet the standards essential for full accreditation. It was providential that JC had experience in "making brick without straw."

McPheeters' three cross-country trips a year to conduct seminary business were often made more difficult by restrictions on travel imposed by the war effort. Editorship of *The Herald* demanded two articles a week. Parish responsibilities added other crushing demands on time and energy: each week required two sermons, a Bible study, a newspaper column and at least six radio talks. In addition, there were ecumenical and denominational meetings, pastoral counseling, weddings, funerals and the usual administrative chores.

McPheeters was sustained in all of this by a God who had

promised "as thy day, so shall thy strength be." His own self-discipline, cultivated and fine tuned in his earlier fight for life itself, was further reinforced by an ability to take refreshing catnaps anytime and under the most adverse circumstances. JC had learned how to live one day at a time, to take one step at a time, to do his best without fretting, and leave the results in God's hands.

The Almighty has a way of blessing in unexpected ways those who put their trust in Him. During construction at the seminary, work was about to come to a halt on a badly needed building for a lack of lumber, a scarce commodity because of the war effort. The situation was made a matter for special prayer by the faculty and student body. Before the end of the week a truck with a load of lumber destined for the far North broke down just five miles from the campus. JC's offer to buy the lumber and thus help the driver solve a problem was gratefully accepted. The needed building continued towards its scheduled completion without delay.

At another time, when a central heating unit was unavailable on the open market, an old threshing machine boiler was found and ingeniously put into use. This also created two new jobs for students, since someone had to fire the boiler around-the-clock.

Asbury Theological Seminary continued to grow as new members joined the faculty and the number of students increased each year. A steady stream of financial support provided for campus expansion and student housing. The American Association of Theological Schools granted full accreditation to the Seminary in 1946. It became increasingly obvious that a full-time president was an imperative.

Decision-making time came again. Thus in June of 1948 Julian C. McPheeters gave up his pulpit in San Francisco to cast his lot fully with Asbury Theological Seminary. He and his wife, Ethel, moved into a modest three-room apartment in the newly completed student apartment house named for "Aunt Bettie" Morrison. The seminary could offer no guaranteed salary–only the assurance that the Lord would provide. His response to the call to become the president of the seminary was an echo of what Henry Clay Morrison once wrote about himself: "The greatest call of my life is the call of Asbury Theological Seminary [which he founded in 1923]. Every other call which I have had culminates in this call."

President McPheeters perceived the training of a Spirit-filled ministry as a mandate of unparalleled importance and urgency.

He underscored this conviction in an editorial: "A cold heart in the pulpit," he wrote, "means death to the pew; we need pulpits aflame" (*The Herald,* November 10, 1948).

The Seminary and the Glide Foundation

McPheeters' 1948 decision to leave Glide Church posed an immediate problem. A pastoral leader with authentic evangelical credentials was a critical need. It soon became evident that the search would have to extend beyond the bounds of the conference. One pastor in Mississippi had a proven track record in tune with JC's tradition. The official board sent a letter to the bishop unanimously requesting that this individual be appointed as the new pastor of Glide Church. At that time segregation in the South had long influenced liberals to believe that "no good thing could come out of the South." This was especially true of Mississippi. Thus the bishop refused to entertain this entreaty as a valid option. Eventually, a prominent Texan was appointed as the pastor of Glide Memorial Church.

This change of pastors, however, did not bode well for the cause of evangelism. The membership at Glide Memorial, in JC's last report in 1948, was "full members: active, 1,430; inactive, 435." The following year the record read, "full members: active, 585; inactive, 1,250."

Significant changes also were in store for the Glide Foundation. From the perspective of one segment of the conference leadership, the time was ripe to take over the foundation. Some in the conference sensed that if they played their cards adroitly the new pastor could be manipulated to lead forth in new directions. If guile were necessary, so be it. McPheeters' successor had automatically taken JC's place on the foundation's board. However, JC continued on as the foundation's president. During the following year a death created a vacancy on the board. At this point the board, following its traditions, nominated a trustee whose name was submitted to the annual conference for election. The unanimous choice for this nomination was Julian C. McPheeters.

This was indeed the process specified in the Glide Trust. However, the trust did not forbid further nominations from the annual conference floor. When the conference convened in Stockton, McPheeters' name was duly brought to the floor. However, something new took place when one member of the conference nominated the presiding officer, Bishop Tippett, to fill the vacancy. Quickly the bishop surrendered the chair to Dr.

Tully Knoles, and a vote was taken. By a narrow margin the bishop was elected.

This strategy did not in and of itself remove McPheeters as president of the Glide Foundation. He presided at the next regular meeting of the board, and opened the meeting with a background summary of the trust, specifically discussing Lizzie Glide's intentions and purposes in establishing it. He also warned that violations of the terms might lead to litigation seeking to void the trust. It was almost as if JC had intuitive powers about what was about to happen.

The same interests that had denied McPheeters his rightful place on the board now had some further unfinished business to take care of. JC had indicated that a sense of obligation to Lizzie Glide would prevent him from resigning the office of president of the foundation. In response, a proposal was made to amend the bylaws so that only members of the board of trustees could serve as officers of the foundation.

This motion passed with only one dissenting vote, that of Dr. Bob Shuler. At this point JC arose and vacated the chair, stating that he counted it a great blessing to his own spirit to have been a board member for so many years. He seemed the only man in the room perfectly composed and at peace with himself. The fact that those for whom he had done the most had taken the lead in his expulsion did not seem to arouse in him any sense of righteous indignation. JC even had the generosity of spirit to keep his dinner engagement with the board before taking his leave for the last time.

Thus his colleagues in the ministry expressed their appreciation for all that Julian C. McPheeters had done. Without him the Glide Foundation would not have had enough financial resources to operate, for it was his leadership in the hotel enterprise that had been the goose that laid the golden egg. "Thanks" for the money power; "no thanks" for the spiritual power seemed to be the attitude of the new leaders of the Glide Foundation.

During the 1940s Asbury Theological Seminary made remarkable progress under the leadership of a part-time president. In 1946 the school received full accreditation by the American Association of Theological Schools. New members were regularly added to the faculty. The seminary's reputation as a leading center of Wesleyan theology attracted an even larger number of students. The new administration building and apartment complex had been built and were dedicated free of debt. Ground was soon to be broken for a chapel and library. A contagious spirit of mission and destiny seemed to permeate the institution during this period.

In his first report to the board of trustees as a full-time president on November 9, 1948, JC had this to say: "We have many reasons for which to thank God and take courage in this great work. It is our profound conviction that God has raised up our seminary for such a day as the present. The need for such a seminary was never greater than today. Our heritage of holiness we must maintain and proclaim along with the other great fundamentals of the evangelical faith. This is why we came into being and this is the only justification of our existence. If we ever lower our standards, and compromise the fundamentals of the Christian faith which gave us birth, we shall go the way that many other seminaries have gone and will no longer have the right to claim the support of the godly and devout people who, through their faith, prayers and contributions have made possible our present success."

During his years of work with the Glide Foundation, JC had developed strong ties between the foundation and Asbury Theological Seminary. From its beginning, the Glide Foundation had invested in the growth and development of Asbury College and Seminary. Indeed, Asbury had long been one of Mrs. Glide's primary beneficiaries. It was not surprising, therefore, that the foundation reflected this same concern, making scholarship grants on a regular basis. A lectureship had been established honoring Joseph and Lizzie Glide. As an endowment fund, the foundation had set aside $200,000 for the seminary. And at a crucial point in campus expansion the foundation made a construction loan of $45,000.

Undoubtedly JC sensed that once he left Glide Church certain changes would come. It is doubtful if he could have anticipated how swift and sweeping these changes would be. Nor could he have known that he would so soon be denied membership on the Glide Foundation Board of Trustees and replaced by others who made no secret of their antipathy toward evangelicalism and its historic meaning.

Swiftly the new Glide Foundation board moved to rescind any and all support for Asbury Seminary. The crowning blow was a demand for the immediate repayment of the $45,000 construction loan. A request for a delay of a few weeks, until the next regular meeting of the seminary's board where proper action could be taken, was summarily denied by the foundation.

Indeed, the foundation board then discounted the note and sold it to a commercial bank for collection. Paradoxically, the bank management exercised the needed compassion and granted the time the seminary needed to arrange to take care of its obligations.

But even this demeaning treatment did not extinguish the loving and forgiving spirit of Julian McPheeters. Let others do what they would; it could not alter his intent to live according to the mind and spirit of Christ.

Controversy in the Halls of Learning

The quest for Truth inherently involves some clash of the old with the new, some need to delineate between appearance and reality, some effort to push beyond facts to their meaning and application. How difficult it becomes, at times, for the academician to live by an espoused credo. Free speech advocates deny the platform to opposing points of view. Research projects are compromised to gain grants. Unexamined assumptions give credence and status to mutually exclusive viewpoints in many areas of inquiry.

Christian higher education has not escaped. A consensus of orthodoxy does not close the door on interpretative diversity: theories of atonement vary; understandings as to the merits of baptism and the meaning of Holy Communion show little unanimity; doctrines concerning sin and the way of salvation lack general agreement; and the problem of evil is so open-ended that the church has hardly been able to agree on even a tentative orthodox understanding.

Not so strangely, then, conflict eventually appeared in the halls of this developing Wesleyan institute of higher learning. What critics and foes of Asbury Seminary could not accomplish, friends almost succeeded in bringing to pass. Having been mauled and battered by the adverse actions of the Glide Foundation Board of Trustees, the president was scarcely ready to face another threatening crisis. But come it did, in the fall of 1950 generated by those whose personal sacrifice and commitment to the seminary could scarcely be questioned. Sincerity of heart and nobility of intent were not enough to prevent an unfortunate drama from unfolding.

Dr. Claude H. Thompson, a cultivated individual and a Christian gentleman, was at the center of the controversy. New to the faculty, he had recently received a doctorate from Drew University. His major professor, Edwin Lewis, was a longtime friend of Asbury and had himself been a victim of partisan theological controversy.

Professor Thompson's crucial mistake seems to have been that he adopted his mentor's solution to the problem of evil as detailed in *The Lash and the Leash*, as the ultimate, rather than one attractive possible solution. At least this is the way some students interpreted the matter. The result of Thompson's pedagogy was to enable certain critics, however mistaken, to charge that he was advocating "metaphysical dualism." Distressed students "carried tales" to other members of the faculty. Even theological students enjoy baiting one professor against another.

Eventually whispers reached President McPheeters that certain unsettling reports were coming out of Dr. Thompson's classroom. The president invited him in for a personal conference. Professor Thompson readily conceded that he had failed to recognize that some students were ill-prepared to deal with his particular presentation of certain disputed theological matters. He was attempting to correct his approach, Thompson said. And he reaffirmed his own commitment to Wesleyan theology. Dr. Thompson further offered to place a letter of resignation in the president's hand at any time the administration felt he had outlived his usefulness as a member of the faculty.

President McPheeters had high hopes that with some adjustments the controversy would subside and Dr. Thompson would be able to continue on at the seminary. However, accusations, rumors and gossip continued. When an implied threat of resignation by nine members of the faculty arose, further action became necessary. A committee was appointed to investigate the matter and report back to the board of trustees. The president and the board could not ignore the honest concern of persons who feared a trend might be developing that could "imperil the historic position and mission of the school."

After intensive investigation, the committee reported that "Professor Thompson's difficulty is mainly pedagogical, rather than any conscious commitment to clearly nonevangelical positions." It was the committee's opinion that he had refrained from explicitly advancing "metaphysical dualism." On the basis of this report the board of trustees voted to delay any action on Dr. Thompson's offered resignation for one year.

Even so, the turmoil did not go away. The faculty schism deepened. Coercion and intimidation appeared to have been employed by principals on both sides of the controversy.

Eighty-five percent of the student body signed a petition in support of Dr. Thompson. Critics outside the seminary, and even some longtime friends, used this opportunity to malign the school.

The seminary was facing a "no win" situation. Regardless of how the board might vote, it appeared the results would be the same: disaster for the institution. Substantial elements of support were almost certain to be lost, the academic credibility of the seminary might be undermined, and the recruitment of students greatly reduced.

When word finally reached Professor Edwin Lewis about what was happening to his protege, Lewis was so incensed that he wrote a nine-page letter castigating the seminary for its actions. Included in it was Lewis' personal threat to see that Asbury would lose its accreditation with the American Association of Theological Schools and the University Senate of the United Methodist Church. The provocation of Asbury's former friend had thus caused him to become an awesome adversary.

The board of trustees became so evenly divided over the matter that any decisive action seemed impossible. This inaction constituted a form of conduct that was also debilitating. Since some action eventually had to be taken, one board member had raised the possibility of Dr. Thompson's voluntary withdrawal with the understanding that he would readily be hired by another institution. However, Thompson did not prefer to run under fire when he considered himself innocent and the charges against him false. Furthermore, he reasoned that to resign at this point would be to place some future professor in similar jeopardy.

As the board of trustees met in prolonged session with no apparent end in sight, a knock interrupted the meeting. President McPheeters was called out. He returned shortly with a statement signed by Dr. Thompson in which he said that in view of the tragic turn of affairs in the seminary it seemed best for him to withdraw from the faculty. Thompson departed with no formal charges against him, no vote of condemnation or censure. Indeed, the board had gone on record as believing wholeheartedly in his moral character and Christian integrity.

The destructive forces released by this bombshell were not long in taking their toll. In 1951 the seminary did indeed lose its American Association of Theological Schools' accreditation. A number of Methodist students were required by their conferences to leave the school. Some who continued to pursue their education at Asbury discovered that they would be required to extend their program in an approved school or be denied admission to their home conference. Other Methodist candidates for ministry dared not risk seeking admission for fear of reprisals by their boards or conferences.

This loss of accreditation could very well have been Asbury's deathblow under a different kind of leadership than that which McPheeters was able to give. Even so, the road back was long and difficult. It began with the president standing before a dispirited board of trustees, some of whom wished to continue the acrimonious debate. President McPheeters relieved the tense situation by accepting personal blame for the crisis: "If I had dismissed this man when I had a chance to do so three months earlier it would have saved the day, but I didn't. I failed." His confession of failure served as a healing balm for the board of trustees, who saw it as the hallmark of greatness.

In characteristic fashion, and without minimizing the disastrous effects, JC looked upon the entire situation with the optimism of Joseph of old: "What others intended for evil, God intended for good." A counselor approved by the American Association of Theological Schools was immediately employed by the seminary to give direction to the task of meeting the requirements necessary to regain accreditation. Goals were set that far exceeded minimum standards, so that the end result was a far stronger school of theology.

The difficult period of restoration lasted for an entire decade. Some true friends despaired. Even so, from a certain perspective, it could be said that critics and foes had unwittingly done the school a favor. Their action resulted in a detailed blueprint for excellence and a more compelling vision of a larger sense of mission and purpose. The transforming power of Christian faith turned darkness into light and defeat into victory. Through the power of prayer, "lean years" became fruitful years for the building of a finer school, an institution some would eventually call "The West Point of World Evangelism."

The Civil Rights Movement

Patience, tact and openness normally served J. C. McPheeters well as an administrator. This was particularly true during the decade of the Civil Rights Movement, which did not leave the campus untouched. Although Asbury Theological Seminary had always had a cosmopolitan student body, with foreign students from every continent, its position regarding racial policies had never been made clear to the public.

The matter came to a focus when a student committee came to the president to express their concern about the seminary community's attitude toward minorities. JC listened quietly, answered the students' questions and left no doubt about the school's solid commitment to openness and inclusiveness.

However, this consultation convinced JC that something more specific must be done to dispel any doubt or ambiguity on this sensitive issue. He went to work immediately with the board to adopt a statement that would clearly set forth the seminary's position. As a result, the board of trustees voted to have the following declaratory statement appear in boldface type on all promotional materials: "Asbury Theological Seminary does not, within the context of its religious principles, its heritage, its mission and its goals, discriminate on the basis of sex, race, national or ethnic origin."

President McPheeters believed that the establishment of a world of peace, justice and unity must rest on the sure foundation that humanity can become "one in Christ." While our society has refused to embrace the totality of the Good News, with such a statement JC attempted to focus seminary attention on being not only my "brother's keeper," but my "brother's brother" as well.

Camp-meeting Evangelist

The president of Asbury Theological Seminary will, by virtue of his office, normally be much in demand as a preacher and Bible expositor. A steady stream of invitations can be expected from local churches, ministerial groups and, above all, the great camp meeting centers across the nation. It becomes important, both for the seminary and the Kingdom of God, that the president be available to accept as many of these engagements as possible.

The camp meeting, it will be remembered, grew out of the great revival which began in the latter part of the eighteenth century and continued into the nineteenth century. It arose as a new approach to deal with the appalling social and spiritual poverty of frontier times. Some have argued that in the twentieth century the camp meeting, as a dated institution, has outlived its usefulness. However, camp meetings continue as a very effective means of evangelism. One great mission board (Sudan Interior Mission), for example, has found that more than one-half of its missionaries have made a major commitment in a camp-meeting type setting.

Early in his ministry JC had been identified as one of

America's most successful camp-meeting evangelists with calls to preach coming from the great camps of both north and south (Superior Park, Hollow Rock, Indian Springs, Camp Sychar). Dozing off during an afternoon preaching service at one of these camps, JC awakened just in time to add a powerful "Amen" to the sermon's conclusion. Later a friend asked the preacher if he thought McPheeters had heard very much of his sermon. The preacher's philosophical reply was, "McPheeters has been dreaming better stuff than I am preaching."

Once settled in Kentucky, JC had to face the problem of what to do about his commitment to the small Redwood Camp in California. The future there was uncertain; conference authorities stood in opposition to the camp and its program. Much time in travel and work would be required to keep Redwood alive; it would close the door on McPheeters' other options. Would it not be better for Asbury if he withdrew and left this matter to others? However, the Inner Voice said, "No!" That settled the issue. McPheeters would remain fully involved with the Redwood Camp at whatever the personal or institutional cost.

In retrospect, this proved to be a decision of momentous blessing for the seminary and the Kingdom. The Redwood Camp has sent a continuing stream of committed students to Asbury College and Seminary. It has likewise provided the seminary with a number of its most generous donors.

A striking example of the value of Redwood Camp to the Kingdom of Christ occurred in 1952. Mrs. Cordelia Thomas was so thrilled and blessed by the program at the Redwood Camp and she deeply longed for her husband to attend. He, Sherman Thomas, was a successful, self-made man content to leave the matter of religion largely in Cordelia's hands. Thomas had 40,000 acres under cultivation and was widely known as "the alfalfa king of America." In addition, he owned a dairy herd, extensive cotton fields and was a shareholder in a cooperative fertilizer plant. Everything Sherman Thomas touched seemed to turn to gold.

Cordelia sought JC's advice and he suggested that she invite Sherman to Redwood Camp for a single day to see what would happen. Sherman Thomas had been around preachers and churches for years, with little effect. Often he had been solicited for financial support of church functions and projects. Occasionally, there were those who invited him to put his name on a church roll. So it happened, caught off guard, he agreed to Cordelia's invitation and came down to the Redwood Camp for a "single day."

McPheeters became God's direct instrument for leading Sherman Thomas into a saving knowledge of Jesus Christ. Never before had any man spoken to Sherman, man-to-man and eyeball-to-eyeball, about his own personal relationship to Christ. Sherman Thomas eventually knelt at the altar rail in an open-air cathedral formed by mighty redwood trees. He arose a new person in Christ. Immediately, Thomas began to rebuild his life in new directions, and to live meaningfully for the glory of God.

Through the intervening years Sherman Thomas became JC's special brother-in-Christ, his sometime traveling companion, and his team worker in the cause of evangelism. Thomas became a member of the Asbury Theological Seminary Board of Trustees and one of its major benefactors. He has been generous in his support of evangelistic and missionary enterprises throughout the world. In the capture of this one person for Christ, God has amply demonstrated how He rewards faith "exceeding, abundantly above all that we ask or think."

Flexibility, Inspiration and Perspiration

Certain situations call for a high level of creative leadership. The Asbury institutions are cases in point. In the early 1920s Asbury College was threatened with bankruptcy and oblivion. A desperate board turned to Henry Clay Morrison as a court-of-last-resort. Morrison agreed to step into the leadership vacuum if the board would give him a totally free hand. To accomplish this he proposed to lease the college from its trustees for one dollar a year. The purpose of this strategy was to give Morrison the necessary freedom to make leadership decisions independently. He was, to put it nicely, never a man who could be content with the interminable slowness of bureaucratic machinery and the petty attitudes and limited horizons so often accompanying it.

As a result, H. C. Morrison is remembered as the individual who not only saved Asbury College but, in 1923, established Asbury Theological Seminary with one bold stroke of his pen. Through the years his preaching and the outreach of *The Herald* often provided the seed-money needed for growth and development. Critics might grumble about his somewhat dictatorial and indeed high-handed style of leadership, but without such it is not likely that there would have been an Asbury College and Seminary.

H. C. Morrison's flamboyant mode would never be characteristic of President McPheeters' administrative style. He followed a more prosaic pattern, while attempting with an open mind to be led by the Spirit. Yet his patience, prayers, and commitment to traditional Christian values developed a unique quality of leadership.

In many ways J. C. McPheeters was always a "loner." He has been described as "having his head in the clouds but his feet on the ground." This imperative need for discipline to cope with a constant overload of work made it difficult for friends to develop the degree of closeness with JC that many coveted. Similar to his spiritual hero, John Wesley, there were simply too many urgent things demanding attention for him to give much time to any one situation.

Preoccupation with great and absorbing issues often made Julian McPheeters appear absentminded. None knew this better than Miss Natalie Gordon, his legendary secretary from San Francisco. He would sit in a contemplative mood while she read letters and documents to him. Ever so often she would say, "Doctor! Are you hearing me?" And he would give an affirmative reply and then surprise her by going on to quote word for word what she had said.

As seminary president, he was fortunate in being able to leave routine and mundane academic affairs in the competent hands of Dean W. D. Turkington. He was equally fortunate to have the astute William E. Savage as business manager. Thus fortified, JC traveled well over 50,000 miles each year by car to maintain contacts, discover new friends and generate financial support needed for seminary maintenance and growth.

Of course, some found fault with this arrangement of a "nonresident, resident president." Others grumbled about his inattention to detail. And not a few were staggered by what they perceived as the impossible dreams of an impractical visionary. Yet who could replace him in raising money and developing a network of concerned, committed, and involved people? McPheeters had little choice but to continue on and do what seemed best for the larger vision of the seminary.

The Asbury community is widely known for its passion for missions. The sun never sets on the seminary's graduates as they serve in every major area of the world. Yet in 1949 there was no scholarship program tailored to the special needs of foreign students. To meet this special need, President McPheeters proceeded to establish the Foreign Students Scholarship Fund. Since each student's situation differed, he thought it better to find sponsors who could underwrite the costs by adopting a specific student. In each instance the lives of both the donor and the student recipient were enriched. The resulting personal relationships often encouraged a better mutual understanding and a deepened appreciation for the Great Commission.

Sometimes there was a need to "bend the rules." One day Dr. J. T. Seamands came to the president with a unique request. In India there was a young man with a voice of operatic quality who very much desired to study music in America. Could the seminary tailor a special musical program and provide a scholarship so that this budding artist could be exposed to the spiritual climate of Asbury? There would be no strings attached, no idea that he might be shifted from music to any other field.

With not a moment's hesitation, JC went to work to see what could be done. Dr. Willard Hallman, chairman of the music department, agreed to provide the necessary special courses. A single telephone call solved the financial problem. Some few months later, Samuel T. Kamaleson was enrolled in the seminary. God, as it turned out, had specific plans for his life. Kamaleson's magnificent singing voice eventually was to become only a part of a worldwide preaching and teaching ministry. Today he is a vice president-at-large for World Vision International. Kamaleson travels the globe and is in constant demand as an evangelist and speaker at ministerial conferences. He is widely known as one of the great Christian leaders of this century. All of this might have been lost without JC's sanctified vision, courage and creative imagination.

On another occasion, a member of the faculty requested help for a Navajo Indian student at Taylor University. He wanted to attend Asbury Seminary but lacked financial resources. Could Dr. McPheeters find a way to help? The answer, as usual, was yes. Fred Yazzi came to Asbury on a foreign student's scholarship. The Navajo tribe did, after all, claim to be a nation! Fred Yazzi was able to become the first fully-ordained United Methodist minister of the Navajo tribe, and he returned to serve his people in New Mexico.

JC's innovative leadership resulted in a number of successful programs during the years of his presidency. First, concern for pastoral enrichment, fellowship and inspiration led to the establishment of the annual Ministers' Conference in 1945. Always held in the most frigid part of winter, it attracts almost a thousand pastors from across the nation. Secondly, when a proposal came for the establishment of a Free Methodist Foundation adjacent to the campus, it had Julian's quick and enthusiastic endorsement. Moreover, he worked out generous provisions for a successful coordinating program. Finally, when plans were drawn up for a student center, JC's concern for higher health standards not only provided for the usual gymnasium, but an Olympic-size pool and a weight-lifting room. Later, through the Martha R. Jones Foundation, he became a pioneer in calling attention to the importance of nutrition as a spiritual responsibility. The foundation has in recent years underwritten the full costs of an annual health lectureship.

In all things showing thyself a pattern of good works . . .
(Titus 2:7, KJV)

6

Facets of Ministry

Prayer: JC's Ultimate Priority

J. C. McPheeters took literally rather than symbolically the scriptural injunctions to "pray without ceasing" and "in everything give thanks." For decades his alarm clock was set at 4 a.m. to mark the start of a four-hour program of prayer, praise and exercise, topped off by a cold bath. Those who have entertained him in their homes, or roomed near him in a motel or dormitory, understand best what this meant.

One young pastor traveling with JC for the first time, and rooming with him as a practical matter of economy, described his experience this way:

> "He closed the day with a brief prayer of thanksgiving for a safe journey and, before I could finish preparing for retirement, he was in bed and in less than sixty seconds in a deep and relaxed sleep.
>
> "It seemed like I had just gotten comfortably settled when a booming voice spoke with resonance and exuberance, 'This is the day the Lord hath made! Let us rejoice and be glad in it!'
>
> "With one eye on the clock, which registered 5:30 a.m., I saw in the light of early dawn a bronzed figure in shorts. With a yell like a Comanche on the warpath, he leaped to the

ceiling and shouted, 'I feel like I could climb a thorn tree with a wildcat under each arm!'

"He had granted me an extra hour and a half of sleep. Now, as one of his physical fitness disciples, it was time to exercise. So I joined with my own stretch exerciser and received some additional instruction as we went our rounds together.

"He not only touched the ceiling that morning—he also touched heaven! Our devotions together were as invigorating and inspiring for the soul as had been the physical exercise for the body."

Occasionally, JC's morning routine appeared redundant. A faculty member was rooming with him for the first time as they shared leadership in a series of meetings. It was a new experience for JC's roommate to have the best part of a morning's sleep disturbed by a barrage of exercises. And only a little less grievous, before his first cup of coffee, to hear the new day greeted with JC's joyous thunderbolt, "This is the day the Lord has made! Let us rejoice and be glad in it!"

Later in the week it became evident that Dr. Mac's energy was outpacing that of his companion. Finally, on the fifth day, the friend had had enough. He admonished JC, "You said that Monday. You said it Tuesday. You said it again on Wednesday. You said it yesterday. Now you have said it again today!" After a short meditative pause, Julian's eyes brightened and he said, "Well, I declare, the Lord's done it again!"

Julian's father had served as a role model for his life of fervent prayer. Later, at Meridian College, JC came to know L. P. Brown, a layman and intimate friend of Sam P. Jones, the famous evangelist. The life of this great prayer warrior provided further convincing proof to him of the power of prayer in every area of human activity.

There are good reasons why "men ought always to pray." Julian McPheeters has expressed it in this fashion:

It is the channel through which men can appropriate the Power that is over and above the forces threatening world destruction. Prayer gives confidence and assurance, brings a sense of certainty and direction, and is a source of abiding joy. If Jesus needed to pray, how much more does sinful, finite humanity.

Prayer is the most creative avenue open to man. It widens

horizons, deepens the experience with God and revitalizes human resources. It removes the impediment of worry. Prayer enlarges planning, stimulates generosity and quickens perceptions of opportunity. Only God knows the accomplishments wrought through prayer. Prayer works when other resources fail!

Little wonder that throughout his ministry he constantly sought ways to encourage others to discover for themselves the efficacy of prayer. The midweek prayer meeting remained a fixture in every local church he served. He sought to enrich and strengthen his own prayer life and others' through twenty-four hour prayer vigils, special days set aside for prayer and fasting, prayer retreats, prayer breakfasts, prayer partners and deeper life conferences.

JC had a special way of introducing silent prayer in public places. A young pastor was having dinner in a restaurant for the first time with Dr. Mac. With the arrival of the first course his booming voice announced, "Let us have a silent blessing!" Every diner in the room heard him. Immediately all conversation around the tables ceased while a self-conscious young minister and his host had their silent grace.

A silent grace at meals in public places was a concession to the sensitivity of others. Time was when only a very vocal prayer would do. Dr. John S. Tremaine laughs about a time in San Francisco when a group met for dinner in a hotel dining room. Mrs. McPheeters, taking note of the soft lighting and subdued conversation, suggested to her husband that a silent blessing would seem more appropriate for the occasion. "All right," agreed Julian in a strong stentorian voice, "Let's have a silent grace." The result, of course, was the very thing she sought to avoid, a quick focus of attention by the entire dining room.

At the time of JC's retirement as president of the seminary, Dean Turkington pointed to his continuing emphasis upon the prayer life of the total Asbury Seminary family as one, perhaps even the most important, contribution in the life of the institution: "The seminary has become a veritable 'school of prayer.' Emphasis on the personal prayer life, prayer cells, prayer chains and nights of prayer has brought very real results in the blessing of God upon the program and world outreach of Asbury Theological Seminary. The seminary has been going forward on its knees."

McPheeters' successor as president, Frank Bateman Stanger,

gave this tribute: "Like Jesus, the Son of God, Julian C. McPheeters is a man of prayer. Truly he follows his Savior along the pathway of prayer. His personal life is fragrant with the incense of prayer. His relationships to others are hallowed by prayer. Especially have I been impressed by the way he has bathed his administrative life in prayer. He has prayed about everything—he prays specifically—he prays expectantly—so 'big in prayer' that on his knees he reaches all the way to heaven."

JC never considered prayer a form of magic or a way to manipulate the Almighty. Nor did he see prayer as merely a matter of form, posture or the recital of a literary liturgy. Rather, prayer was a "hot line" to God; a conduit for listening as well as petitioning; an instrument for expressing praise and gratitude. He understood that "prayer changes things" by changing people. Such people, in turn, are used of God to change things.

Therefore, it is not surprising that JC took a dim view of prayers read from a book or written out in advance to be delivered as a performance. Writing to a former parishioner, June 10, 1963, he replied to a direct question on the matter.

Such prayers are usually lacking in dynamic vitality and life-giving spontaneity for the uplift and inspiration of the congregation. A minister does not usually climb the heights into the heavenly places of inspiration in prayer on the ladder of a written prayer. Such heights are ordinarily scaled under the inspiration of the Holy Spirit at the time the prayer is uttered. The Holy Spirit may use the vehicle of written prayer in preparation for the high hour and moment when the pastoral prayer is offered, but when the high hour has arrived for the pastoral prayer to be uttered, the Holy Spirit should not be circumscribed nor limited by a previously written prayer. . . . We seek to develop this type of praying here at Asbury Theological Seminary.

Perhaps that is why through the years JC's prayers touched so many persons. Gaile Morris, retired professor of Hebrew at the seminary, was near her one hundredth birthday when she wrote: "When he prayed, the heavens opened, and God answered by fire. No one could hear him preach without knowing there was deep prayer life prompting it." Ralph and Orlean Beeson have written: "We look forward and feel blessed by his short devotional and prayer with us."

JC's friends have frequently commented on their responses to JC's prayer life.

"I am always inspired when I hear him preach or prayer."

"He has inspired me to greater faith in the power of prayer and the practice of God's presence."

"You know that he lives so close to God that it seems to draw one closer just to visit with him and especially to have him pray."

Joe Hale, general secretary of the World Methodist Council, has known JC in a personal way through a mutual commitment to the International Prayer Fellowhip. He once observed: "He leads us to the Throne of Grace, not in a backward, timid way, but as one who knows his Lord and converses with Him daily."

In handing out diplomas at commencement, JC would often say to young graduates: "Son, be a man of prayer." This concern was reflected in an interview that appeared in *The Herald* (March 1976). He was asked, "What advice would you give to those entering the ministry today?" In reply, he said: "My first advice is to keep humble. Humility will be maintained through prayer and fasting and the Holy Spirit. My second counsel is to be sensitive to the needs around you. Spend much time in the closet of prayer, but likewise spend much time in the marketplace where the needs of the world are to be found."

One of JC's basic concerns was for the maintenance of a proper balance between the horizontal and the vertical dimensions of life. These must become an integrated whole, he believed. McPheeters argued that "prayer and the marketplace was the pattern used by Jesus. He would talk with His Father through the night hours, and then He would be back there in the marketplace with the people."

McPheeters' approach to every problem was through prayer. On a certain occasion, when the seminary badly needed a new faculty member, JC found the man he wanted teaching in another institution. He called a prayer retreat and invited a select group of seasoned men of prayer to gather at a motel in Tennessee for three days of earnest prayer. Evidently the Lord heard, for something happened out West which motivated Dr. Delbert Rose to accept McPheeters' invitation for him to join the seminary faculty.

JC believed in praying specifically: "Lord, Thou knowest we need $27,500 more to complete this project. Thou knowest those individuals who are able to make these funds possible. We ask that Thy Spirit motivate them to respond to this need." Then, having prayed, he would wait expectantly for the mail.

At times, those around him regarded such idealism and trust as a bit out of touch with reality. As one colleague expressed it: "This characteristic is so pronounced that sometimes I have wondered if he were almost unrealistic about certain very real situations. Perhaps all of this is an authentic witness of true faith."

JC's reputation as a man of prayer began early in his ministry. In the formative days of the prayer breakfast movement, which got its start in San Francisco, McPheeters was the only clergyman invited to share in what was otherwise an exclusively lay effort. When Dr. Harry Denman and Helen Kim launched the International Prayer Fellowship, he played an active role. Later, he helped promote prayer vigils for peace in Vietnam. And he joined in organizing America's Bicentennial Fellowship of Prayer.

All who knew him can testify that JC sought to put into practice what he preached. Professor W. C. Mavis reports: "There were times when I discussed my work or some other problem with Dr. McPheeters and near the end of the interview he would bow his head and start 'talking to God' as simply and naturally as if the Almighty were physically present in the office. I left such interviews feeling that three persons had really been present: God, the president and myself."

Another seminary faculty member, professor Donald E. Demaray, states: "The chief relevance of a great life like Dr. McPheeters' is, in one word, modeling. But we must add another word, prayer. Only God knows the powerful effect of his prayers. I once asked him to pray about a specific challenge I faced. Days later he shared with me his almost astonishingly accurate answer."

Model for Fasting

Fasting serves a legitimate function in the life of the spirit. Jesus regularly went aside for times of prayer and fasting. Fasting has an inseparable link with prayer throughout the New Testament. In so far as fasting helps sharpen mental faculties and enhance a variety of physical functions it moves the individual toward a revitalized spirituality. Nowhere is this more evident than in the realm of prayer.

For years JC made fasting a normal part of his life. At least once each week he observed a day of abstinence from food. And in special times of retreat he sometimes extended the practice over several days. When he was a pastor, JC set aside the first Friday of every month as a day of parish prayer and fasting. As a seminary president he made frequent calls for full days of prayer and fasting on behalf of the school and its mission in the world.

McPheeters never regarded fasting as a work of merit to earn credit with the Almighty. For him, it was not something to boast about. True to the Bible mandate, such observance should be kept imperceptible to those around the one fasting. Benefits accrue primarily to the individual, and the ultimate values are known only to God. "And when you fast," said Jesus, "do not look dismal . . . that your fasting may not be seen of men but by your Father who is in secret; and your Father who sees in secret will reward you" (Matthew 6:16-18).

Reliance on Scripture

John Wesley once said: "I want to know only one thing—the way to heaven; how to land safely on that happy shore. God Himself has condescended to teach the way; for this very end He came from heaven. He hath written it down in a Book. O give me that Book! At any price, give me the Book of God."

Julian C. McPheeters stood firmly in the noble Wesleyan tradition of those who believe the Bible not only is true, but it is "living and active." He saw it as history and personal verification combined. His was an unwavering belief that in the Bible was the authentic Word of God for time and eternity. He believed that the distortions of eisegesis and higher criticism, coupled with self-serving forms of exegesis, might deface but not destroy the divine authority of Scripture. JC regarded the Bible as the cornerstone of Christian truth, never to be compromised or prostituted.

JC's attitude toward difficult passages in Scripture was much like that of Dwight L. Moody. In reply to a question on this very matter, Moody said in substance, "Do exactly what you do with fish bones; put them aside and eat the meat." Applied to the Bible this would mean to put into practice first what you do know and understand, then further enlightenment may follow.

Two men greatly influenced JC's thinking and appreciation of Scripture—Professor Charles Erdman of Princeton and Dr. William H. Evans, noted Bible expositor and preacher. On five different occasions Dr. Evans spoke at Glide Church for week-long Bible conferences. And it was Evans who gave JC a whole new vision about the value of memorizing Scripture by chapters and books. With typical determination and dedication, he began a memorization program that gave him a mastery of much of the New Testament and significant portions of the Old Testament.

Throughout his life, McPheeters regarded the Bible as a rock upon which to build an unmovable and victorious faith. He declared with the psalmist of old: "With my whole heart I seek thee; let me not wander from Thy commandments! I have laid up Thy word in my heart, that I might not sin against Thee. Blessed be thou, O Lord; teach me thy statutes" (Psalm 119:10-12).

This Bible, which enabled Luther to bring to birth the Reformation and sparked the Wesleyan Revival in England, was for Julian McPheeters a bastion for faith and the practice of the Christian life. Without it there could be no spiritual awakening. Above all it remains a peerless mediator of the resurrected and living Christ, a road map for daily living, and a guidepost for eternity. Its teachings inspire godliness. Its promises provide healing, hope and renewal. Its pathway offers a highway of holiness. Its truths provide the answers to the highest hopes and deepest longings of the human race.

"A man of one book," J. C. McPheeters remained throughout his life a devout reader of the Word, practitioner of its precepts, and fearless proclaimer of its fundamental message. In this respect, as in so many others, he was, indeed, a follower of his Methodist forefather, John Wesley.

Evangelism

Jesus' final commandment to His followers was, "Go and make disciples of all nations"; or, as the King James version states it, "preach the gospel to every creature." The Early Church took this mandate seriously and were eager to witness and share their faith. For this reason, the church grew and its influence was felt throughout the then known world.

In later centuries the energies of the church were caught up in apologetics, battling with heretics, codifying doctrines, and filling the political vacuum of a decaying Roman empire. Eventually the world began to set the church's agenda. The church became entangled by the world's cultural milieu and thus its sense of mission waned. As late as the eighteenth century there seemed to be a consensus within the church that "saving the heathen is God's exclusive business and He will do it in His own good time." William Carey's journey to India in 1793 finally launched the modern missionary movement.

Specifically, critics have called the missionary endeavor "spiritual colonialism," pointing with scorn to forced conversions, ridiculing cultural impositions, bemoaning racial triumphalism, and accusing missionaries of undermining indigenous customs by way of a "rice Christianity."

The missionary enterprise from New Testament times to the present has, of course, made mistakes and suffered failure. But even these failures should be critiqued within the historic and cultural context of the day. Missionaries have always been more than mere "Bible thumpers." They took with them the seeds of liberty and humanitarianism, the ideals of equality, social justice and kindness. Especially in modern times missionaries have built schools and hospitals, liberated women and children, improved agriculture, and waged war against poverty, ignorance and bondage.

J. C. McPheeters was throughout his ministry an ardent advocate of fulfilling The Great Commission through an energetic program of evangelism and world missions. He sensed that as Methodism's concern for evangelism waned, so too would the interest in missions grow cold and probably move in more secular directions. McPheeters was awake to the implications of such voices as that of William Ernest Hocking whose 1932 report, "Rethinking Mission," advocated a syncretism of the world's great ethnic religions. McPheeters argued that the justification for both evangelism and missions properly centered in Christology, specifically the answer one gave to the crucial question, "What think you of Christ?" If Christ were only a good man, a great teacher, a symbol of virtue, an inspiring example, then abandoning evangelism and the missionary enterprise does not profoundly matter. But if, on the other hand, He is who He claimed to be, the promised Messiah of Scripture, the Incarnate Son of God, Deity, the Divine Invader, then these issues matter intensely.

Standing in the vanguard of those who acknowledged the essential Deity of Jesus Christ, JC preached this doctrine from the pulpit, and supported it in the life and program of the church. While some theological seminaries were dismantling departments of missions, McPheeters led the way as Asbury Theological Seminary sought to strengthen and expand its evangelism and missions program. As Methodism worked at reducing its missionary force, the seminary continued to produce a constantly renewed stream of volunteers. The very recently dedicated (February 1984) E. Stanley Jones School of Evangelism and World Mission is, in some sense, a fulfillment of President J. C. McPheeters' longtime vision for Asbury Theological Seminary.

Christianity itself, as JC so often emphasized, is the product of missionary effort on the part of the Almighty: "God had only one Son and sent Him as a missionary into the world." Those believing this have volunteered themselves, left the comforts of home for alien lands, immersed themselves in the language and customs of other people, shared the message of love on the cross, and demonstrated its meaning through sacifice and service, even unto death itself. When Adlai Stevenson returned home after traveling through Africa, he said that the thing that impressed him most was ". . . the graves of missionaries to be found in profusion throughout the land."

JC's Physical Fitness Program

McPheeters insisted that the Bible has a high regard for the physical body as "the temple of the Holy Spirit." In writing to the church in Corinth, a city famed for its debauchery, Paul declares: "Do you not know that your body is a temple of the Holy Spirit within you, which you have from God? You are not your own; you were bought with a price. So glorify God in your body" (1 Corinthians 6 :19,20).

He came to believe for this reason alone that Christians should have a concern for physical fitness. Anything that usurps the control of the Holy Spirit over God-given desires, appetites and instincts is considered wrong, even sinful. This has been the primary motivation for crusades against alcoholism, drug abuse and the tobacco habit, or any life-style that undermines health. Gluttony is a perversity that transforms the necessity to eat into the grossness of "living to eat." Obesity and anorexia are the results of choices which have come under condemnation as a violation of God's laws for health. Spiritual fitness cannot be divorced from physical fitness.

Critics delight in pointing out that the Bible says "bodily exercise profiteth little," using it as a rationale to ignore the need for physical fitness. This, however, is but another example of how a phrase can be taken out of context and given a meaning not intended by the writers of Scripture. Paul, writing to young Timothy, is talking about the relative merits of the physical and the spiritual. "Train yourself in godliness; for while bodily training is of some value, godliness is of value in every way, as it holds promise for the present life and also for the life to come" (1 Timothy 4:8).

In the process of regaining his health, JC made some biblical discoveries and came to certain conclusions about health which influenced his life thereafter. Like most farm boys, Julian had inherited a sound body that was further strengthened by good food, hard work and spiritual nourishment. Health was something he took for granted, a fact that enabled him to work long hours and burn the candle at both ends and in the middle. Not until his battle with tuberculosis did he begin to understand the importance of nutrition, exercise and adequate rest.

The move to San Francisco forced a radical alteration in JC's program for physical fitness. His excursions to hunt and fish were necessarily limited by factors of distance and time. His sometime commitment to golf was more a chore than a delight.

His interest in weights came quite by accident, the result of my having acquired that previously mentioned pair of hand dumbbells when I was in my teens. Once he started using my dumbbells, JC was always on the lookout for new and better ways to exercise. He discovered Noe's Exercise Rubbers, with their graduated resistance of 27 to 250 pounds, and used them for many years. But the ultimate in physical fitness tools came with the manufacture of the Exer-Geni. A simple rope mechanism, scientifically developed by a college athletic director, it provides for both isotonic and isometric tensions, from 10 to 410 pounds. For years he pulled the maximum each day. Indeed, he became an enthusiastic salesman for the product, with all profits going into a health program at the seminary.

To make his message on health more convincing, he began to put on demonstrations as evidence of the lasting worth of exercise. Young people were intrigued, especially when their athletic peers could not duplicate his feats.

Numerous stories recount the McPheeters exercise regimen. A conference at one of the Kentucky state parks assigned Dr. Mac to a room immediately above one occupied by two elderly ladies. Unaware of JC's early morning practice of vigorous exercise, these ladies didn't get much sleep after 4:00 a.m. Later in the day they complained publicly that someone had been "stomping" heavily on the floor above them. Persons in the know chuckled but never said a word. They just knew better than to room too near the culprit.

JC received a unique invitation from Greenville College in Illinois in February, 1974. The department of physical education and the department of philosophy and religion had been working together for two years to explore the relationship between spiritual commitment and physical fitness. They wrote him, "Your name came up as the ideal exponent of this. You are, therefore, invited to the campus to model for our students the two very powerful emphases of your life: A godly desire for sanctity, and a commitment to the building of a strong body as stewardship of life."

His visit met with enthusiastic response from the student body. Later, the athletic director wrote and said he would like to see this repeated on other college campuses. "I can get you as many invitations as your time will permit," he went on to say.

Physical fitness had not been a fad for JC, nor exercise a gimmick. A theology of wholeness and the goals of perfection must make a place for exercise, nutrition and recreation. Over the years JC inspired multitudes to take a greater interest in health care as a vital part of the Christian stewardship of life. As one faculty member wrote, "Dr. McPheeters' emphasis on health has helped me personally and thousands of others. I take exercise and nutrition more seriously because of his enthusiastic support and modeling of the principles of wholeness."

JC espoused exercise in order to "add years to your life and life to your years." He often closed one of his demonstrations with a bit of verse for skeptics.

I'M FINE

There's nothing the matter with me,
I'm just as healthy as I can be.
I have arthritis in both knees
And when I talk, I speak with a wheeze.
My pulse is weak and my blood is thin,
But I'm awfully well for the shape I'm in.

I think my liver is out of whack,
And I have a terrible pain in my back;
My hearing is poor and my eyes are dim,
Everything seems to be out of trim.
The way I stagger is a crime;
I'm likely to fall most any time.
But, all things considered, I'm feeling fine.

Arch supports for both my feet,
Or I wouldn't be able to walk down the street.
My fingers are ugly; stiff in the joints;

My fingernails impossible to keep in points;
Complexion is bad, due to dry skin,
But I'm awfully well for the shape I'm in.

My dentures out, I'm restless at night,
And in the morning I'm a frightful sight.
Memory's failing, head's in a spin,
I'm practically living on aspirin,
But I'm awfully well for the shape I'm in.

Now the moral is as this tale unfolds,
That for you and me who are growing old,
It's better to say I'M FINE with a grin
Than to tell everyone of the shape we're in.

—Author Unknown

Health Education

The first grandchild to grace the McPheeters' household was a cause for great joy and celebration. Indeed, in a fashion rather uncharacteristic of him, JC was so excited at his grandson's baptism that he scooped enough water out of the baptismal font to almost drown the lad.

Without any hint of what was to come, this birth would prove to be the key that captured JC's deep interest in the field of nutrition. Martha R. Jones was a member of Glide Church, having retired in 1941 after a distinguished career in the field of research in nutritional diseases. She had become the first woman to serve as an assistant in the department of physiological chemistry at Yale University, where in 1920 she received her Ph.D. Over the years she did research at the University of California Medical School in San Francisco, Queens Hospital in Honolulu and at the U.S. Naval Academy.

Dr. Jones gained international recognition for organizing and directing the Ewa Plantation Health Project in Hawaii. The experiment offered indisputable proof of the important role of nutrition in combating childhood diseases and tooth decay.

It was natural for Dr. Jones to take more than a passing interest in JC's grandson. Young parents are naturally nervous with their first baby and willing to do anything that might benefit the child. They welcomed Dr. Jones' advice as she shared her expertise with them.

As ties of friendship deepened, Dr. Jones mentioned her dream for a wider dissemination of the lessons learned about the health benefits only good nutrition could supply. Her plan was to try and do this through one of the great medical schools of America. It was at this point that the writer happened to suggest that Dr. Jones might do well to look beyond secular agencies. A school such as Asbury Seminary was sending graduates forth to serve all over the world. Many would live and work all their lives among the poor and undernourished. What better way to broadcast this message and have it reach those in need?

In the course of time, this seed-thought would germinate and lead to the establishment of the Martha R. Jones Foundation for Health and Education at Asbury Theological Seminary. Only the concern and tenacity of Dr. McPheeters, however, kept the idea alive and brought the dream into reality. There was a general attitude of indifference, and some hostility, toward the whole idea. Lectures on health and nutrition seemed incongruous in a theological institution.

Thus on April 25, 1961, a charter was issued for the Martha R. Jones Foundation, and Asbury Theological Seminary added one more dimension to its concept of wholeness and broad concern for the human family. With it came the establishment of a health center and clinic.

One of JC's major aims was to extend the years of active service for missionaries and ministers. He considered it a sin against God and humanity when such leadership was struck down in the prime of life, since the world sorely needs physically fit, socially adjusted, intellectually prepared, Christ-filled men and women on the firing line for God. For this reason the Jones Foundation would sponsor an annual health lectureship and bring in a renowned authority in nutrition to inform and interact with students and faculty.

Perhaps the most obvious and immediate benefit has been the development of a day care center. This service was made available to all without regard to race, creed or national origins. Subsidized rates are much less than those charged outside the community. It has been a vital witness of Christian concern for the well-being of home and family. It has made it possible for student wives to continue with schooling and mothers to work outside the home.

Throughout his career as seminary president, JC sought to develop new and larger facilities specifically designed for program needs at the seminary. He knew, too, that a more adequate endowment was necessary to fund future needs. Few doubted that, as long as Julian McPheeters remained at the helm, these goals would be reached.

McPheeters left no doubt that he wanted strong, vitally alive men and women to carry the Gospel out into the world. Physical vitality was an essential ingredient of this profile. Often he would declare from the pulpit: "I want Asbury Seminary to produce real men to preach the Gospel. The namby-pamby Milquetoast personality has no business trying to declare a Gospel of power that can transform the world!"

He was a consistent practitioner of what he preached, constantly exploring and testing new products and nutritional prescriptions. From E. Stanley Jones' green "alfalfa pills" to capsules of red pepper, from ginseng tea to Gee-Gee molasses, from raw vegetables to protein powders and the pollen of bees, JC experimented with concoctions, often mixed together in a blender, that were supposed to be beneficial to health.

First-time roommates were always in for a surprise. Here is how one man described his experience: "The contents of his suitcase were different from any I had ever seen before. After extracting his stretch exerciser, dumbbells and handgrips, he produced a strange looking gadget something like a space rocket. What it proved to be was a blender for mixing up health cocktails. He then took out a large can of protein powder mix, a can of Gee-Gee blackstrap molasses, and a box of powdered milk. He put a combination of these, along with water, into the blender, turned on the motor and within thirty seconds had the drink he wanted. Removing the cover, he gulped the contents down with relish, explaining how delicious and energizing it really was. Then it was time to prepare for bed."

This companion concoction should have been around in the days when JC hauled a brace of sun lamps around in the back seat of his car, so as not to be denied the health-giving benefits of the sun's ultraviolet light. However, one thing must be said: whatever he did certainly worked for his benefit. He exuded the radiance of good health, a contented mind and a triumphant faith until the very moment of his death.

Healing

The community in which Julian McPheeters grew up knew as much about "snake handling" as it did about "faith healing." Prayers, of course, were offered on behalf of the ill, but not as a substitute for doctors and medicine. It was generally assumed that medical knowledge was part of God's gifts to humanity which had once been locked away in His world, but now discovered and made applicable to human need.

JC's battle with tuberculosis brought a new and personal knowledge about the role of faith in the healing process. His own faith had served him well, and he was the recipient of many prayers on the part of family and friends. Later he would declare, "I would not be here today without a praying father."

Thus, it was easy for him to applaud the growing rediscovery and emphasis upon the role of faith in healing. However, as practitioners began to multiply and "faith healing" turned into an art form, he had a growing concern over abuses and exploitations. He considered it a violation of scriptural teaching, as well as a cruel hoax, to turn faith into a compelling form of magic, to make all disease and illness expressions of unbelief and a lack of personal trust in God.

McPheeters summarized his basic understanding of "faith healing" in a letter to a woman in Bismarck, North Dakota, dated July 20, 1977. In it he considers what he believed to be five basic scriptural categories:

First, there is the fact of instant healing, something repeatedly demonstrated in the miracles of Jesus.

Second, there is the fact of a process to be followed as a prior adjunct to healing. The story of the ten lepers would be a case in point. Jesus told them to go and show themselves to the priest. They were "healed as they went"; the reward for obedience and faith. An Old Testament illustration would be the story of Naaman, the leper. Elisha, the prophet, told him to go and wash seven times in the Jordan River. Only then was Naaman healed.

Third, there is the miracle of a Divine remedy such as that offered to Isaiah when told by God to place a cake of figs on the boil of Hezekiah. As a result, the king's boil disappeared.

Fourth, there is the sufficiency of Divine grace. This is the miracle that gives strength and fortitude to endure an adversity we are compelled to live with, such as Paul's "thorn in the flesh." Why? In Paul's case, it may have been the only way to maintain humility and the needed dependency upon God for the tasks ahead.

Fifth and finally, there is the miracle of "the triumphant crossing." From the moment of inception, humanity starts a universal and inescapable journey toward death as an intrinsic part of finitude and the wages of sin. Sooner or later all die. Yet for Christians death is not an ultimate tragedy. Rather, it is the doorway to a new and more abundant life, an ongoing existence in the presence of God where His perfect will is done, and where there will be no illness, pain, separation, sorrow or death. "To be absent in the flesh is to be present with the Lord!"

The key in "faith healing" for JC was the matter of commitment, a faith that leaves in the hands of God the details and the unfolding pathway to come. The ultimate issue must always remain, "Not my will, but Thy will be done." Under these terms he had no hesitation in holding services for healing and anointing the ill with oil.

One day a friend who lived two states away called and asked JC to come to the bedside of his wife who was so ill the doctors had despaired for her life. The one possible hope lay with very high-risk surgery. At the bedside, JC anointed the patient with oil according to scriptural practice, quoted some of the great promises of God and prayed. His final word was, "Remember to keep it committed." The wife went on to surgery and eventually recovered. Later she wrote: "Dr. McPheeters' prayer seemed to penetrate the roof and the glory of heaven came down and filled my soul. As I was being taken into surgery his words kept ringing in my ears, 'Keep it committed.' Since then this lesson in faith has guided me through other crises in life."

The timing of God is also held to be an important matter in the healing process. A brilliant young surgeon in Lexington, Kentucky, was stricken by a life-threatening viral infection caused by a freak accident; a colleague had nicked his surgical glove during an operation and infection followed. The resulting illness was not only severe, but seemingly beyond any known medical help. He was forced to abandon his medical practice. In time things became so bad he had to give up his home and move the family in with his parents. Each passing day seemed to be a countdown for death.

Then one morning a devout Wilmore, Kentucky businessman, John Fitch, heard the voice of God say: "Go get Dr. McPheeters and take him to see this young doctor so he can tell him the story of Divine healing that took place in his own life." The immediate result of this visit was to give the young surgeon a new understanding of what it means to trust in God and to enter into a real fellowship with Him. From that day on the illness began to recede. In a matter of weeks he was fully recovered and able to resume his medical practice. The events clearly constituted a miracle of healing faith.

This doctor was not lacking in a Christian background or a personal faith. Home influences had been of the very best, for he was the son of the president of Asbury College. Legions of people had made him the subject of prayer. In his hour of travail what he needed was the light of faith from one who had himself been near death's door and conquered.

Fundraising Strategy

The ability to generate financial resources for the Kingdom of God was an outstanding characteristic of JC's ministry. Had he devoted these same talents to the business world, there is little doubt that he would have become a man of substantial wealth. It was in the role of seminary president that this talent reached its zenith. One observer declared, "Dr. McPheeters has truly been a money raiser for Asbury Theological Seminary. I feel he has done more than all other persons put together in the matter of publicity for the seminary and actually raising money." The significance of his work is underscored by the condition in which he found Asbury when he became president. A faculty member, looking back over forty years of history, commented, "One can almost say that J. C. McPheeters built Asbury Theological Seminary. Its buildings, its faculty, its financial structure is indebted to him almost alone. He probably will never be replaced in this phase of his ministry. He had no predecessor and will probably have no successor in this indispensable role of growth."

A lay member of the board of trustees described the impression JC made. "He was a living illustration of what they were building at Asbury—preachers of holiness. He didn't have to say it; they could see for themselves. He told it from the heart. People believed him, had confidence in him and they laid down the cash." In another way, the same quality of JC's is highlighted by a bishop: "His great success at raising money grows out of a spiritual authenticity that creates an explicit trust in his integrity. A positive attitude and spiritual concern developed confidence to the point where almost an automatic desire is generated making people anxious to respond."

As an example, in the spring of 1955 the seminary was facing one of its perennial financial shortfalls. Furthermore, Julian's wife was suffering from terminal cancer. When asked what was needed, the business manager replied, "$20,000." Where to turn in such a crisis? Where JC always went, to the secret closet of prayer. After much tarrying, God brought to his mind the name of a banker in Corbin, Kentucky. JC hastened to the telephone, detailed the current crisis and made a request for a ninety-day note. "What a coincidence that you should call," said the banker. "I sold some securities and just got the money a few days ago. Send me the note and I will forward the $20,000." Later, the note was returned as a gift to the seminary. In telling this story JC would close with this jocular punchline: "You can't get a better loan than one with no payback."

JC knew, of course, that integrity needs to be wedded to proven methods and principles to keep the pipelines full and the flow of fiscal support uninterrupted. "I regard raising money," said Julian, "like growing a crop." There is a time to plow and a time to plant, a time to water and a time to cultivate and, finally, the time of harvest. All of this demands intelligence, patience, sensitivity and understanding.

The first concern with prospective donors, JC saw, should be the person and not the gift. Sensitivity to spiritual opportunity and human need must transcend any quest for support. Essential ingredients for achieving this would include his fellowship, finding common grounds of identification, and maintaining contact. He must avoid being negative or judgmental; instead, he would always respect donors' personal desires and special needs.

The personal ability to put these principles into practice has given Julian McPheeters an amazing record of success with people in every category of wealth, education and social status. A pastor who has observed him in action on numerous occasions wrote, "Dr. McPheeters' gift of fund raising on a one-to-one basis is the greatest that I have ever seen. He put it all on the spiritual basis of helping the man he was interviewing simply by befriending the client in the most sincere manner."

JC's initial contact with many prospects came by way of a mutual friend, a pastor, or an alumnus of the school. People of wealth are often cynical, having been exposed to a constant barrage of appeals for support. This mood of cynicism was expressed by one lawyer with an opening greeting, "Well, I suppose you're looking for money!" "No, sir," came JC's reply, "I'm looking for men!" Before the visit was over the attorney had apologized for his defensive greeting and JC had laid the groundwork for future contacts and eventual support.

On a first visit to a doctor's office, JC noticed a Weatherbee Rifle on the wall and admired it. This opened up an exchange about guns and hunting. The doctor ended up accepting an invitation to join JC on his annual deer hunt in the foothills of the Big Horn mountains of Wyoming. The personal rapport that developed over the years not only generated current scholarship support, but a place for the seminary in the doctor's estate plans.

Hunting and fishing interests have proven to be fertile grounds for making friends for the seminary. JC's sharing of common interests with prospective donors and friends of the seminary went a long way in building bridges of understanding and confidence. A fishing partner went home and sent in a gift of $100,000; a hunting companion left $500,000 in his will for the school.

Sharing a rancher's roundup of cattle and showing an interest in the business of ranching started a friendship that one day netted the seminary $1,250,000. And the interesting thing is that those who got "fired-up" about the seminary usually had a friend or two whom they wanted JC to meet.

Yet JC believed that the church should never despise the small gift! Getting people involved is the important thing. It is general practice for initial giving to be made in modest amounts.

JC had great respect for small gifts and was quick to express his gratitude for them. He enjoyed telling about an experience The American Bible Society had. A woman in Texas responded to their routine mass mailing with a two-dollar gift, which was duly acknowledged with appreciation. For each of the next five years she made an identical contribution. Then one day "out of the blue" she sent in a check for $1,100,000. One seminary donor's initial gift over twenty years ago started with $5. The following year the gift grew to $25. In a few years the gift was up to $25,000 and eventually reached $120,000. Despise not the small gift!

Of all the variety of ways to solicit funds, the most productive is not to ask at all. As an Alabama businessman put it, "The remarkable thing about our financial support of endeavors Dr. McPheeters was interested in is the fact that not once has he ever asked, or suggested, we give one cent." And from another businessman in Wyoming comes this testimony: "He never used any high pressures in soliciting support for the seminary."

Such technique seems to breed a group of donors who not only give with enthusiasm, but somehow seem to feel that Dr. McPheeters has done them a great favor in opening up this avenue for Christian stewardship.

In 1949 the opportunity arose to apply JC's financial principles in the creation of a development office for the seminary. A then-recent graduate came to Dr. McPheeters greatly disturbed by the fact that the school's growth and potential was being compromised by a lag in generating financial resources commensurate with that need. "I feel that I want, that I must, help my school in some way," said Robert Fraley, "but I cannot abrogate my call to preach." The instant response was, "Young man, that is just what we need. Go preach, and as you go, tell our story."

Thus the words, "Go tell our story," became the key which opened the door for Robert Fraley's fifteen-year career as development officer for Asbury Seminary. The program unfolded in keeping with JC's commitment to fund raising as a spiritual ministry. The constant focus was on a person's need to become a better steward of what God had entrusted to him. Every prospective donor and faithful supporter of the seminary was continually covered with a mantle of prayer and concern. Thus the development process became a ministry rather than a mercenary operation. In time, nine field representatives were kept busy criss-crossing the nation keeping in touch with constituents and making new friends.

JC remained active in every phase of the development program. One of the most valuable aspects of his leadership was the recruitment and training of field representatives. His striking success here was his ability to convince men of the possibility of the task. Lowell O. Ryan, a United Methodist pastor and former district superintendent from Texas, is a case in point. "For eleven years I have served as a field representative for Asbury," wrote Dr. Ryan. "He showed me how to discover prospects and taught me how best to influence people to do something for the Kingdom and the school."

Perhaps a final word should be said about JC's ability to raise funds through the taking of a public offering. He grew up in a day when this practice was common in the life of Methodist churches. At the end of the harvest it was customary to resort to this technique to meet conference obligations, balance the budget, or provide needed funds for repairs and improvements. It was an occasion for excitement and fun as the preacher sought to "extract" what was needed, and then it was put into the public record what individuals were willing to give in support of the Lord's work.

Seldom is this method used today except in revival and camp

meeting circles or rural communities. The pastor faces a general hostility toward any pressure or public disclosure of giving. The average church member tends to support the church like he pays club dues or makes payments on a charge account. Even so, at least part of the constituency looks to the public offering as the indicator of need and the motivator of response. Persons not allergic to generosity and sacrifice seem to enjoy the excitement generated by a drama that takes on the characteristics of a medieval folk play.

JC always succeeded in this arena of the public offering. A straightforward statement of need, sprinkled with homespun humor couched in colloquial terms, enabled him to obtain whatever sum of money might be needed. When McPheeters was taking one of his famous offerings at a camp meeting, he started at a thousand dollars and gradually lowered the ante until he reached $25. As he asked for raised hands a young girl punched her companion and said in a loud whisper, "Don't move! Last year he was taking the offering and I scratched my head and it cost me $25."

Without doubt, the public offering approach is an endangered species. And well it might be, as the "old guard" vanishes. Perhaps this occurs, too, because tithing seems to be God's basic plan for funding the Kingdom.

JC never was apologetic in matters of church finance. He was well aware that Jesus made money and its use a primary topic of conversation. It is one thing to have possessions; it is quite another thing to be possessed by possessions. Love knows no limits save its own capacity to share and to serve. And until people know how much Christians care, they will care little for how much Christians know.

The Altar Call

Preaching for a verdict is inherent in the Gospel message. In Methodist circles the altar call became an instrument to encourage a positive response to Christ's invitation to follow Him—a symbol of the surrendered life. God's new covenant in Christ called for personal commitment. Paul summarizes it in this fashion: "Present your bodies as a living sacrifice, holy and acceptable to God, which is your spiritual worship. Do not be conformed to this world but be transformed by the renewal of your mind, that you may prove what is the will of God, what is good and acceptable and perfect" (Romans 12:1,2).

J. C. McPheeters used the altar call throughout his ministry, making it an integral part of his preaching. If Jesus sent his disciples forth as fishers of men, then this was one way to "draw the net." This did not rule out other approaches or make them any less valuable or authentic. He had no quarrel with those who did not use the altar in this fashion if other methods and techniques were employed to achieve the same goals. However, he did view the use of the altar as an opportunity to reach the casual visitor and the random stranger in a way not readily available through the use of other methods.

Any situation is tragic when the church makes no effort to present the claims of the Gospel and seek definite personal decisions for the living Christ. Without such personal commitment, there exists neither obligations nor benefits. When, for example, we take out insurance, buy a house or car, or accept a charge card, we sign on the dotted line and enter into contractual agreements of mutual responsibility. In a far more profound way, responding to an altar call is an initial step in the Christian's life.

JC never made the altar call an exclusive highway to heaven. He always emphasized it, though. Beyond the altar call, he also employed the Fisherman's Club, visitation and one-on-one personal work. He believed in small group Bible studies, prayer cells, retreats, summer camp programs, deeper life conferences, radio and, later, television for reaching out and providing avenues leading to a Christian commitment.

Sharing the Christ of the cross and the empty tomb was as natural for JC as for believers in the Early Church. He coveted for others the joy and happiness he had found. Like Philip he would seek out Nathaniel and announce, "We have found the one Moses wrote about, Jesus of Nazareth." If prejudice and bigotry against the faith surfaced (can any good thing come out of Nazareth?), he would respond with the spirit of Philip, neither argumentative nor judgmental: "Come and see." This spirit guided JC in the use of the altar call and all of the other methods he regularly used to call persons to vital Christian commitment.

Beyond his public preaching ministry, JC was a soul-winner in many other ways. In particular, his hunting trips were special opportunities for sharing his faith. By way of example, he hunted antelope near Gillette, Wyoming, for more than twenty-five years. For ten of those years he had had the same guide. On one trip his two hunting companions found it necessary to shorten their hunt. Since his time had been paid for, JC suggested to his guide it be used for conversation and an opportunity to get better acquainted. He had been praying for this man and his wife all these years. This seemed to be the opportunity he had been praying for God to give him. The guide invited JC to his home for a meal. As they visited together, the wife admitted she had at one time been a Sunday school teacher, but a split in the church had left her so disillusioned and embittered she drifted away. She voiced a desire to "get back to God." God's timing was perfect, and the man and his wife found new joy in Christ. The rewards of hunting and fishing JC's way can transcend the satisfactions of bagging a trophy or getting a limit of game.

Sometimes good intentions can put a preacher like JC on the spot. Once, urged to drop by the house to meet a husband who merely tolerated his wife's "religious fanaticism," JC was greeted by the man with, "Well, how much do you expect to get out of me?" This was, of course, a sad commentary upon the reputation of the church. "I'm not interested in your money," replied JC, ignoring the innuendo, "I'm interested in you." Weeks later JC made a return visit to the same home. This time the husband, with a very different attitude, warmly welcomed him at the door. He could hardly wait to get inside before exclaiming, "McPheeters, I want to be a Christian." The initial visit had become a catalyst for the Spirit's working. And a new day dawned for both the husband and his wife.

Then, again, there are times when a preacher falls under the conviction of his own message. And this is the way it should be; every messenger of God stands under God's message. In 1982 JC was invited to preach at a fifth Sunday rally of seventeen United Methodist churches in Overton County, Tennessee. His theme that day was, "A Revival in Overton County."

During the course of this message JC fell under conviction. God seemed to say to him, "You are part of this county. You have a recreational home here. What are you going to do?" Almost at once he thought of a service station operator where he had purchased gasoline from time to time. Now, with impaired eyesight and a body wracked with cancer, the owner spent his days in a chair near the front door, while his wife managed the business.

The next day JC started out for this service station, praying that there would be no customers around to interfere with his visit. But alas, when he arrived the place was a beehive of activity. Then suddenly everyone vanished and he found himself alone with his man. Together they talked about the love of God and the hope of a life to come. JC read some of the great promises of God. The station owner reached out a hand, calloused from long years of hard work, to seal his commitment to Christ. JC prayed, and, almost as if on cue, his closing amen was followed by an influx of customers. But the way had been prepared for a "triumphal crossing."

The Bible says, "He who winneth souls is wise." This being the case, Julian McPheeters must be numbered among the wise men of this age.

With long life I will satisfy him, and show him my salvation.
(Psalm 91:16, RSV)

7

"Retirement" Years

Shifting Gears

In May 1962, shortly before his seventy-third birthday, Julian C. McPheeters stepped aside as Asbury Theological Seminary's president. The institution he had saved from demise was then growing in strength and vigor. The annual budget had grown from $15,000 to $547,000; student enrollment increased from 90 to 322; faculty expanded from 5 to 19 full-time professors. Total assets had spiraled from $218,933 to $6,309,063. Fifteen hundred alumni were in active service throughout the world.

A land acquisition program had greatly expanded the size of the campus. New buildings included the H. C. Morrison Administrative Building, The Bettie Morrison Apartment House, Estes Chapel, the Luce Prayer Chapel, the Ely-McIntire Hall for women, twenty-two duplexes for married students and a central heating plant. Plans were on the drawing board for a library and a student center.

Endowed chairs included the McCreless Chair of Evangelism, A Chair of Missions, the Frank Morris Chair of Christian Doctrine and the Butler-Valade Chair of Biblical Theology. The student scholarship program had greatly expanded, with aid to foreign students alone topping $65,000 a year. The Ministers' Conference had become a fixture, and The Freitas Lectures firmly established.

Pardon Me, Sir

A testimonial service honored JC in Estes Chapel on May 17, 1962. Expressions of appreciation took many forms. Letters from alumni might well be summarized by a paraphrase of Scripture: "You are our letter of recommendation, written on our hearts, to be known and read of all men; and you show that you are a letter from Christ delivered by us, written not with ink but with the Spirit of the living God, not on tablets of stone but on tablets of human hearts" (2 Corinthians 3:2,3).

The board of trustees named him president emeritus, conferred on him a lifetime membership on the board, and continued occupancy of his apartment as long as he wanted it. The chairman, Dr. C. I. Armstrong, paid tribute to him as a man of decision and determination, a person of devotion, discipline and dignity. He praised McPheeters for demonstrating the meaning of New Testament Christianity, one who "could do all things through Christ who strengtheneth us." The gift of a TV set followed with the vain suggestion that "now you might be able to stay home once in awhile and watch it."

Professor George Turner announced that a special committee had established the Julian C. McPheeters Missions Foundation to provide student scholarships and point the way for the eventual establishment of a School of Missions. Dr. Turner also led in raising funds to commission a life-size oil painting of President McPheeters. This beautiful painting, at the request of Mr. Sherman Thomas, has found its permanent home in the lounge of the Sherman Thomas Student Center.

But perhaps nothing pleased JC more than the provision made for his continued involvement in the life of the school by being named director of development. This enabled him to continue the task of raising the five million dollars needed for the next phase of plant expansion. Relieved of academic administrative duties, he was free to travel the highways and skyways as needs dictated. And travel he did, as he shifted into a new high gear with a life-style offering greater freedom of options for service to the seminary and the larger church as well.

"Every man desires to live long," wrote Jonathan Swift, "but no man would be old." In a youth-oriented culture the words of another observer are especially germane: "To know how to grow old is the master work of wisdom and one of the most difficult chapters in the great art of living." Few will doubt that Julian McPheeters mastered this great art. This is so much so, in fact, that one can apply the term "retirement" only in a facetious way to mark the years that followed society's mandated retirement birthday. At a time when most men would be content to "fish and loaf," he turned leisure years into rewarding years of continued public service.

Learning to Ski at Seventy-Three

In 1962, at seventy-three and in retirement, JC found himself with three grandchildren who were very skilled at water-skiing. Although he found a great deal of enjoyment in pulling them behind his boat, that alone was not good enough. He confided in a friend that he wanted very much to learn how to ski. As a result, Frank Harris invited him to come to Lake Alatoona, Georgia, for ski lessons, following McPheeters' engagement as evangelist at the Indian Springs Camp.

"First, we will go bass fishing," said Harris "Then I will teach you to water-ski." After an early-morning catch of ten bass, it was time for lessons. As one expects with beginners, the initial attempt to get up ended in failure. A second try succeeded, with JC grinning and laughing like a schoolboy. An exhilarating morning at skiing came to an end with a call to lunch on the morning's catch of bass.

The initial bloom of this achievement began to fade when his grandchildren graduated to a single ski. Now JC, too, wanted to meet this new challenge. He began by kicking off one ski. But this was only a temporary phase of the transition. He longed to master the craft of getting up on one ski. Learning to slalom proved to be a more difficult chore than anticipated; he was seventy-six before mastering the technique. And what did he then want for Christmas? A wet suit so he could extend his ski season into early spring and late fall.

Thirteen years later a local newspaper, intrigued by reports of an eighty-nine year old gentleman slaloming for twenty-five miles at a time on Dale Hollow Lake, sent a reporter and photographer to investigate and verify the story. The picture story and write-up that followed was featured in a Nashville, Tennessee daily. Later the story of the nearly nonagenarian skier was picked up by Ski Magazine and by newspapers across America and Europe.

The Herald

Henry Clay Morrison conducted revival meetings in Glide Memorial Church on five different occasions. On his last visit he spent a great deal of time discussing his plans for Dr. McPheeters to succeed him as editor of The Herald. His closing word was,

"You ought to be good for another twelve years." Guess who had a long wait at the gates of paradise.

McPheeters' name first appeared on the masthead as editor on April 15, 1942. *The Herald* continued to function as a house organ that promoted the special needs of Asbury Seminary, but its primary message remained the proclamation of "free salvation for all men and full salvation from all sin."

One of the most dramatic stories of the paper's spiritual impact started with a gift subscription that a friend in Georgia sent to a neighbor who was not a Christian. For weeks this neighbor tossed the paper aside without even removing the wrapper. Then one rainy day, unable to go into his fields, and for want of something better to do, he opened a copy of *The Herald* out of idle curiosity. What he read that day aroused his interest, and he began to look forward to the arrival of each new issue. In time, this exposure to the Gospel led him to become a Christian.

This Georgian convert shared his new-found faith with family members. The ultimate result was that two sons entered the ministry, while another son and daughter went to the mission field, one to the Orient, the other to South America. Just one more story of scattering the seed and what God can do with it to bring about a harvest.

For some decades the annual Thanksgiving and Christmas offerings were major sources of income for the seminary. Through *The Herald*, friends and constituents responded with such generosity that the impossible became possible.

Since *The Herald* had no mandatory retirement age, JC continued on as editor. For many years it was the financial life-line for Asbury making possible the seminary's survival.

In July 1975, the time had arrived for JC to relinquish his role as editor, to close another chapter in his book of life. He had served *The Herald* for almost forty-six years, including six as a contributing editor and thirty-three as editor. In parting, he wrote, "*The Herald* and its readers are dear to my heart. Much of my life in prayer and spiritual concern has been invested with you. I am now an octogenarian of fourscore and six years. My first editoral in April 1942 was on the subject, 'After Easter, What?' I was thrilled in that first editorial in the glory of the Easter hope for the future. As I write my farewell after more than 33 years as editor, I am now thrilled in the anticipation of a new advance for *The Herald*."

As usual, the changing of the guard was not an occasion for mourning, but a time for praise, gratitude and the sounding of a note of optimism and hope for an even brighter future. *The Herald* was, therefore, no longer employed as an instrument to generate financial support. It became a house organ prepared largely by the seminary staff to reflect theological concerns, biblical insights, and to deal with devotional life and the Christian's response to the world around him.

The last edition of *The Herald* under JC's editorship featured a picture of him halfway sitting on the edge of a desk. Someone later pointed out that it might well depict the character of the man. "Dr. McPheeters' nature is symbolized by both the strong brick wall behind him and the soft curtain at his right."

Living with Disappointment

It is doubtful if any question was ever asked more often of President McPheeters than, "What do you think of what has happened to Glide Memorial Church since you left?" Persons looking for a negative, judgmental and bitter response were regularly disappointed in JC's reply. He always said that he did what he could while he was there and that the record of his achievement during eighteen years as pastor could not be erased. McPheeters stated, late in life, that he prayed for his successor, The Reverend Cecil Williams, every day.

JC did not believe that any person should live life in bondage to what others do or fail to do. "Vengeance is mine," saith the Lord, "I will repay." Life has more worthy goals than self-defeating motives of revenge or retaliation; move on about the task to which God has called you. Leave the rest in the hands of the Almighty. About all anyone ever elicited from JC was an admission that he was "disappointed in the course of events at Glide Memorial."

A review of the record may help all to understand why. This abbreviated summary of the more recent years of the Glide story is based on written documents and public speeches.

On December 1, 1929, a Deed and Declaration of Trust was drawn up and signed by Lizzie H. Glide, J. W. Sims and A. T. O'Rear, the latter two as president and secretary of The Glide Foundation. It was notarized by R. H. C. Proffitt and recorded in Book 1966 of Official Records, page 1, of the City and County of San Francisco. The intent of the trust is clearly outlined in a paragraph to be found on page three of the document:

That the purpose of this trust is to provide for the preaching and teaching of a true evangelistic gospel based

129

on the fundamental doctrines of the Christian Faith, and all preaching and teaching of any kind whatsoever at said evangelistic center and training school, or ever promoted or maintained through the medium of this trust, shall be in conformity with the established doctrines of the Methodist Episcopal Church, South as set forth in the Twenty-five Articles of Religion of said church, and in Watson's Institutes and John Wesley's sermons, and more especially the doctrine of the deity of Jesus Christ, His atoning sufferings and death for the whole human race, His bodily resurrection from the dead, His ascension, and the work of the Holy Spirit in teaching, convincing, and witnessing to the pardoning power and sanctifying influences and powers; and that nothing shall ever be preached or taught through this trust that shall controvert any of said doctrines.

On page eight of the trust provisions are set forth for the property to revert to other parties "in the event of a violation of any of the conditions herein before set out."

One of the primary concerns Mrs. Glide had for San Francisco was the establishment of a school like Asbury. It was a desire she expressed repeatedly, but which was denied for a lack of adequate funding. The proposal for a Summer Institute staffed by Asbury Seminary professors was set aside for fear it might interfere with the larger dream. She would wait for an accumulation of more funds. In the meantime she would continue her longtime support for Asbury.

Mrs. Glide served as treasurer of the Glide Foundation throughout her lifetime. No funds were ever expended which did not first have her approval. Twice she wrote sizable checks to help meet debt retirement needs of Asbury Seminary. On another occasion she gave the seminary securities in the amount of $20,000.

The Glide Foundation also began to establish more permanent forms of continuing support for Asbury Seminary. On October 13, 1942, the "Lizzie H. Glide Lectureship" was established with an annual appropriation of $150. On October 13, 1943 an annual stipend for $2,700 was authorized for the "Joseph and Lizzie H. Glide Chair of Theology and Philosophy of Religion" at the seminary. The following year (1944) the foundation made a loan of $45,000 to assist in a building program at Asbury. A resolution by the board of trustees, October 8, 1946, set aside $200,000 as an endowment for Asbury Seminary.

"Retirement" Years

By 1951, however, a revamped board of trustees, with McPheeters finally ousted, rescinded all support for Asbury Seminary and in early July sent a letter demanding full and immediate payment of the $45,000 construction loan, due July 21, 1951, plus $900 of accrued interest. Since the seminary was unable to comply on such short notice, the Glide Foundation then discounted the note to a commercial bank for collection.

The legal firm representing the trustees of the Glide Foundation in all these matters wrote that the action taken "was not actuated by any matters of personality or absence of good will towards the seminary but that it has been induced solely by their desire to faithfully and fully carry out their duties" and "in view of the needs of the funds of the foundation for the primary purposes of the trust."

The record which follows must, therefore, be understood to be definitive of how "to faithfully and fully carry out the primary purposes of the trust."

First, one must see how the foundation had come to see its mandate from Mrs. Glide in contrast to its earlier statement of intent. It is set forth in a statement of Purpose and Activities, found on page 86, in "The Foundation Directory Edition Three," edited by Marianna O. Lewis and published by the Russell Sage Foundation, New York, 1967: "Primarily an operating foundation for experimenting in social and organizational change and discovering new structures and relationships through which the church can relate effectively to the San Francisco Bay Area; emphasis placed upon ecumenical and interdisciplinary effects, the training of churchmen for mission in urban culture, and the encouragement of indigenous leadership among minority groups and groups with specialized need."

At the same time the Glide Foundation reported financial data for the year ending 31 May 1965 as follows: Assets, $2,882,027; expenditures, $227,204, including $193,905 in grants and programs.

Second, one must note the comments of Reverend Cecil Williams, senior minister of Glide Church, speaking for himself as to details of his theology, philosophy and the "celebrations" that take place in the church. Most of what follows he shared in 1969, when he addressed a Convocation on Worship held in St. Louis:

"In every service at Glide Church we embrace one another. We kiss one another. We smell one another. We feel one another.

"The chairman of my official board is an admitted homosexual. And why not? This is one way for a person to find his sexual identity.

"Most of our people believe in the communal life. I have not married a single couple at Glide who were not already living together.

"One qualification for our secretaries at Glide is that they be sexy and wear mini-skirts. If a woman is sexually desirable, why not tell her so?

"We had one of our girls who had given birth to a child out of wedlock stand before our church and tell the inner joy of having a baby without moral inhibitions.

"People become stimulated in our church happenings. We believe in people doing their thing and doing what they want to. Several have become so stimulated . . . they have disrobed. One young man came to church covered only by a blanket. During the service he walked up front and threw his blanket down and stood there totally naked. If I had been there at the time I would have walked over and patted him and said, 'Man, what a beautiful body you have!' Why? Because for me there is nothing dirty or sinful about nakedness.

"Glide Church sets the tempo for the night clubs. We do our own thing and then the night clubs of the Bay Area pattern after us."

According to Cecil Williams, Glide Church does not ask for personal faith in Christ. Rather, he improvises and asks, "Are you committed to God's revelation in history and how He is acting at the present time?"

Third, one should examine some of the programs and activities sponsored by Glide Church. It has promoted and encouraged financial support for the Black Panthers, the Angela Davis Defense Committee, the United Farm Workers, the Pit River Indians, Gay Liberation, the Free Speech Movement, the Cuban Revolution, and Anti-Vietnam War Protests. It helped to found and support: 1) The Council for Religion and the Homosexual, an organization that seeks to gain acceptance of homosexual and lesbian conduct as viable, alternate life-styles; 2) Vanguard, a group formed to help male prostitutes and drug addicts; and 3) Citizens Alert, to aid "victims of police harassment and brutality."

In 1967, Glide Church hosted a weekend "Happening" sponsored by the Artists' Liberation Front. It drew large crowds of young people, from drag queens to members of Hell's Angels.

Naked men and topless belly dancers moved easily around a sanctuary filled with clouds of incense, the smell of pot, the sounds of drums and horns, all against a mood background of candles and flashing lights. Downstairs, this event provided sex films and improvised beds for the stimulation and release of sexual passion. All of this, along with dancing, singing and the chanting of Hindu mantras, the church intended to use to build bridges of understanding between polarized groups. Dubbed "The Invisible Circus," it proved to be highly visible for the peripatetic voyeur. This new ecumenism was brought to a premature halt by public authorities because of massive violations of fire and safety regulations. It took $6,000 to repair the property damage already inflicted.

In May 1971 one of the first homosexual "marriages" took place in Glide Church. In 1972 Rabbi Abraham L. Fineberg was installed as "Rabbi in Residence," while go-go-girls danced in celebration of the occasion. Waving a cane, the gift of Ho Chi Minh, Rabbi Fineberg said: "I am a revolutionary. I'll always be one. I am backing Angela Davis for her moral courage and intellectual freedom representing all peoples on earth. I hope to be of service by combining these ideals with those of 'Chairman Jesus'!" In 1974 Glide Church played host to a convention of prostitutes who proudly wore medallions with the inscription "'74 the Year of the Whore." Pulpit guests over the years have included such people as Jane and Peter Fonda, Dick Gregory, Angela Davis, Sammy Davis, Jr. and Saul Alinsky.

And what has been the reaction of United Methodist leadership? Well, Bishop Donald H. Tippett, under whose leadership "Pandora's box" was opened, has praised such innovations as "evangelism at its best." If silence gives consent, then it would seem that subsequent Episcopal leadership and The Council of Bishops concur in such an assessment.

Once these new directions were firmly in place, one attempt was made to invalidate the Glide Trust. The court battle was lost in a maze of legal technicalities and misinformation.

Cecil Williams seems to glory in the role of a rebel-liberator. "Everybody," he says, "has to have hope that things are getting better. My thing is to tell them it's so. In the old church they called it saving people. We call it liberating."

Near the end of his life John Wesley issued this warning: "I am not afraid that the people called Methodists should ever cease to exist, either in Europe or America. But I am afraid lest they should only exist as a dead sect, having the form of religion without the power."

Paul wrote to Timothy with these words of exhortation: "Preach the word, be urgent in season and out of season, convince, rebuke, and exhort, be unfailing in patience and in teaching. For the time is coming when people will not endure sound teaching, but having itching ears they will accumulate for themselves teachers to suit their own likings, and will turn away from listening to the truth and wander into myths. As for you, always be steady, endure suffering, do the work of an evangelist, fulfill your ministry" (2 Timothy 4:2-5).

Herein lies the measure of greatness of Julian C. McPheeters' life and ministry. If there are times when silence speaks with greater eloquence than words, it is a fact Jesus demonstrated in the halls of a kangaroo-court. Blind eyes, deaf ears and closed minds make speech an exercise in futility.

"To Walk the Second Mile"

The ability "to walk the second mile" demonstrates character and independence from the faults and failures of others as conditions of conduct. The life of Julian McPheeters has been remarkable for his ability to incorporate these concepts into daily living. He has done so with such consistency that even some friends have misinterpreted it as a sign of "weakness" and a "lack of realism." The long term results, however, have proven otherwise.

If some of the incidents that follow seem contradictory to the spirit of Julian McPheeters, it is only because he himself lived above them and would never on his own have mentioned such matters. However, if one is to make the record complete, and to allow others to sense with greater clarity how consistent has been JC's ability to apply his principles without wavering, regardless of circumstances, the facts must appear.

In the eyes of a secular world, JC had ample grounds to be hostile and negative toward the church. It had left him ill and stranded for over three years without financial assistance. Authorities have, at times, been less than honest with him in matters of appointment. His evangelical theology accorded him minority status and minimal recognition among his peers, who were busy redefining historic Christian equations. Yet there was never a whisper of complaint from him. Such matters he ignored and took in stride. His call was to serve the Master and to follow where truth lead.

When Glide Foundation trustees and conference colleagues showed their appreciation for all he had accomplished by shameless acts of intrigue and deliberate expulsion, he accepted it without bitterness or dissent. What others might do was their own responsibility. It mattered not that even those personally most indebted to him failed to stand by him, even entering into the conspiracy. He would continue to be a friend, as if nothing divisive had taken place.

Asbury Theological Seminary and Asbury College face each other across a main street in Wilmore. They share a common heritage, common goals, common purposes. It is, therefore, important for the two institutions to work together. Dr. Z. T. Johnson, president of the college, was noted as a strong-minded man with fixed opinions. On occasion, he expressed a certain disdain for theological education. In his opinion, it was better to bypass seminary and opt for a Ph.D. Over the years numerous occasions arose when the president of the seminary might have taken offense and had good reason to engage in confrontation, but JC refused to take the bait.

Never ruffled, never impatient, always congenial and brotherly, JC continued to behave as an understanding friend. In the end he became ZT's best friend. For years they lived across the road from each other. And when JC returned home from a trip, ZT would be the first to welcome him, even coming over to help unload the car. Cooking was a hobby with ZT, and his most frequent guest was Doctor Mac. About a year after ZT died, his good friend looked across the road at a darkened home and said in rather a plaintive voice, "I surely do miss Dr. Johnson." Here is a constructive lesson in human relationships. Both men might have been denied the riches of friendship and years of association if it had not been for Dr. Mac's refusal to fight fire with fire.

The faculty conflict which surfaced in the seminary and almost destroyed the school was not allowed by JC to result in a legacy of rancor. He admitted his mistakes and learned a lesson. Prayer was the prescription for healing and wholeness, JC the role model of faith, vision and fortitude. He found no time for acrimonious debate. As Jesus declared: "We must work the works of Him who sent me, while it is day; night comes, when no one can work" (John 9:4).

William E. Savage, longtime business manager of the seminary, had these words of praise for Dr. McPheeters at the time of his retirement as president. "In all experiences, whether pleasant or unpleasant, I have never known Dr. McPheeters to act in a way which I thought was unchristian. He has exemplified the Christian spirit in all respects in the administration of the work of Asbury Theological Seminary. It was his close walk with God which has enabled him to meet all circumstances, both favorable and difficult, with strength and with Christian maturity."

A school with the uniqueness of Asbury Theological Seminary makes any change in leadership and administration a matter of profound concern. Julian McPheeters, like H. C. Morrison before him, had the good fortune to select his own successor, a man who could augment his skills and build further on the foundations he and others had laid. Frank Bateman Stanger came from a very successful pastorate in New Jersey and served as executive vice president for three years prior to his installation as the third president of the school.

No one could have asked for a more avid supporter than JC. Indeed, Dr. George Turner recalls two different occasions after his retirement that JC, reflecting on his twenty years as president, remarked, "One of the most important contributions I made for the well-being of the seminary was when I recommended to the trustees that my successor should be Dr. Frank Bateman Stanger." Although some things would change, as was to be expected, he never had anything but praise for his successor. He was delighted now to be able to devote full time to undergirding the financial needs of a flourishing institution.

Not many people retire as head of any organization, remain active in its program, and live to see an immediate successor serve for two decades. Indeed, a youth-oriented society does not encourage those forced to retire by virtue of age to remain active, effective, forward-looking and appreciative. To accomplish this was but another hallmark of the uniqueness of JC's life.

However, it is by no means easy to live for long in close relationship with a living legend such as J. C. McPheeters, whom many regarded as a saint. Hence, as time went on, tension mounted. One painful episode that seems to symbolize this tension at its peak occurred when JC, returning from a fund-raising trip, discovered that he had been assigned to a new office in a building far removed from seminary life. To add a certain insult to injury, JC's carefully indexed library had been unceremoniously dumped into boxes and stashed in the hallway. Paradoxically, the thing that seemed to trouble McPheeters most was that this move imposed conditions that might handicap him in his work for the seminary. Some of his friends were less sanguine and more realistic. Their protests were so vigorous that new office space was provided along with restored support services.

I offer these aspects in the story of J. C. McPheeters' life because they have helped me, as his son, to see with even greater clarity the stature of my father, Julian C. McPheeters. He was a Christian gentleman who consistently put the principles of his faith into practice. As I have mentioned previously, there were several times that JC had more than enough reason to seek retaliation, an avenue of response that might well have been taken by a man of lesser character. Yet retaliation did not appear to enter his mind as an option. What Jesus said of Nathaniel seems applicable to him: "Behold, an Israelite indeed in whom there is no guile!" (John 1:47). Whatever his faults, then, JC could never be accused of being devious or vindictive.

Until the time that the divine summons to "enter into rest" came to him only a few months prior to this writing, J. C. McPheeters continued his labors on behalf of the Kingdom of Christ and on behalf of Asbury Theological Seminary. He pursued the work assigned to him with the spirit of the Apostle Paul who wrote: "But I do not account my life of any value nor as precious to myself, if only I may accomplish my course and the ministry which I have received from the Lord Jesus, to testify to the gospel of the grace of God" (Acts 20:24).

A Prophet with Honor

Prophets without honor in their own country are legion. Home folk can see the warts and wrinkles, witness mistakes and failures. This, blended with natural propensities of envy, greed and pride, often reduces public expressions of esteem. And nowhere would this likely be more true than in small towns where secrecy and anonymity cannot prevail.

From 1948 until his death in October 1983, JC lived in Wilmore, Kentucky, walked its streets, shopped in its stores and was under the watchful eye of the town's population. He lived as he preached, a man of humble grace, unshakable faith, projecting a joyous optimism. And through the years he won the affection and commanded the respect of the community-at-large. Not that many thought him perfect. He had his idiosyncrasies, but his sterling qualities of integrity and saintliness made criticisms seem irrelevant.

JC was the only citizen surprised when Mayor Harold L. Rainwater proclaimed May 26, 1979, as "Dr. J. C. McPheeters' Day for the City of Wilmore." "His zeal and zest for life and the church have made him a tremendous influence," commented the mayor. "We have made him the city's official chaplain."

137

Billy Glover, a native-born son and local businessman, expressed what many felt: "I have remarked many times that the man I have the most faith in in Wilmore is Dr. McPheeters. If I had one hour to live and they would say, 'What do you want to do?' I would say, 'Go get Dr. McPheeters to pray for me.' I haven't run into one person who had a word to say against him. I'm proud of him."

Every community seems to have someone on its doorstep, mild-mannered, a jack-of-all-trades, who can't hold any job long because of a problem with alcohol. Paul Fuller had this role in Wilmore. JC befriended Paul, took him fishing, and over the years provided odd jobs when he was down on his luck. Since he had to be away a lot, he made arrangements with the local restaurant to provide meals for Paul any time he needed them and to charge them to JC's personal account. Later JC would extend this help to cover medical bills. Throughout all of these years JC's one basic desire was to see his friend find new life in Christ. His prayers were answered when not long before he died Paul became a Christian. Such acts of compassion and kindness did not go unnoticed in the community.

John Fitch is owner of the local IGA grocery store, the biggest operation of its kind in the state, despite the fact he refuses to sell tobacco or beer. Fitch was such an admirer of Julian McPheeters that for years he insisted on taking him into Lexington to catch his planes and then meeting him when he returned. He did this cheerfully and gladly at all hours of the day and night, in rain, sleet and snow. And when asked, "Why?" John Fitch's simple answer was, "For the joy of being with such a man of God."

New Horizons

"The world has no place for a negative Christian!" This note, sounded in JC's final chapel message as active president of the seminary, might well serve as a capsule summary of the spirit pervading his life. As a result, he was not intimidated by the aging process or impending "retirement." These fears, so common in an era that worships at the shrine of youth, did not trouble him. He continued to see every turn in the road as an opportunity for greater things to come.

This spirit was reflected in a letter, in June 1974, to a colleague who stood on the threshold of retirement: "I commend to you the encouraging words of the prophet Zechariah, 'It shall come to pass, that at evening time it shall be light.' You have only entered the gleam of the evening. As one who is twenty-three years your senior, I commend to you the new and richer experiences with our Lord which are possible as we travel in the glow of the sunset of life toward the sunrise of the Eternal Tomorrow, where the sun never sets."

A "heavenly affinity" developed between Julian McPheeters and E. A. Seamands, a Methodist missionary two years his junior who retired from India in 1958. Their bond of friendship began back in 1925 when EA's father was converted under JC's ministry in Tucson, Arizona. In later years, when these two old warriors of the Cross met on the streets of Wilmore, or elsewhere, they doffed their hats and sang together:

> "Christ gives joy unspeakable and full of glory,
>   full of glory, full of glory.
> Christ gives joy unspeakable and full of glory,
>   And the half has never yet been told."

Mercifully, the Bible speaks only of making a "joyful noise" unto the Lord. This rite became a standard ritual. They met and sang their "theme song" while others smiled and received a special blessing. The last time they sang "Christ gives joy unspeakable" was within hours of JC's death.

Even so, the waning years of life involve valleys of infirmity and dark clouds of loneliness. Several years following the death of his wife, Julian wrote a friend, "In the departure of my dear wife I have learned the meaning of the lonely road, and yet not lonely because I have had the unseen presence of Him who walked with men on the way to Emmaus on the first Easter morning."

The thinning ranks of one's friends and the end of years of friendship also provide moments of grief and pain. Yet these fleeting moments soon vanish in the warmth and sunshine of God's love. One is reminded of the Christian who died and went to heaven. From the narthex of paradise he was given an opportunity to view a map of his footprints through life's pilgrimage. At the point of his commitment to Christ he noticed the start of a dual set of footprints. However, as he traced his pathway there were occasions when only one set of footprints was in evidence. Surprised at this, the newly arrived pilgrim said, "I thought You promised to be with me all the way!" To which Christ answered, "My son, the single set of footprints is where I carried you across the rough pathways of life." Julian McPheeters knew beyond doubt how true this was. "I can . . .

through Him" was the foundation on which he built his life.

A friend in town once inquired about his periodic visits to the local cemetery. "I don't go to weep," was his reply. "I stand by the grave of my beautiful wife. I look across the graves of Henry Clay Morrison, John Wesley Hughes and other great soldiers of the Cross and remind myself I have to be ready. Some day I will join this great host."

There are those who see Julian McPheeters' life as the embodiment of three major careers: effective pastor, remarkable educator, and miraculous fund raiser. Full commitment to Christ and his normal positive attitude toward life itself explain the ease and grace with which he had made each new transition. No one ever heard him say, "The day returns and with it comes its petty round of irritating cares." His note was always positive, joyous, exuberant and optimistic as he affirmed each new day in thunderous tones: "This is the day the Lord has made! Let us rejoice and be glad in it!"

Man of God Award

On February 18, 1982, Religion in Media bestowed upon Julian McPheeters a Golden Angel as the first recipient of their "Man of God Award." Their citation gave recognition to his conspicuous qualities of Christian discipleship and moral leadership:

Author of a score of books, hundreds of magazine articles, for 33 years editor of *The Herald*, he was a pioneer in the field of radio ministry. Evangelism crusades have taken him from South America to Africa, through most of Europe and the Holy Land. Successful pastor, he was ever sensitive to the temporal needs of people and the moral climate of community life. He organized, for example, the first church-sponsored agricultural training program for farmers in his native Missouri. His three-year battle with tuberculosis, made without any church financial assistance, turned him into a book salesman and an insurance agent for a time. When health was regained he returned to his pulpit despite other alluring financial offers. He signed the Articles of Incorporation for Asbury Theological Seminary in 1931. Eleven years later he became its second president and over a twenty-year period laid the foundations which make it now the ninth largest seminary in the United States and Canada. Still water skiing, on one ski, at 93 he is an eloquent symbolic expression of his unconquerable way of life. The chief lesson of life? The will of God is the highway of victory! God knows his business. His work is to abound more and more. There are no limits.

A BIBLIOGRAPHIC INTRODUCTION TO THE PUBLISHED WRITINGS OF JULIAN CLAUDIUS MCPHEETERS*

Throughout his long, distinguished professional career, much of Dr. McPheeters' thinking found expression in printed form. His weekly column and other articles appeared regularly in *The Herald* which he edited from April 8, 1942 until June 11, 1975. While pastoring, he wrote a weekly newspaper column, had printed his daily radio talks for distribution to listeners upon request, and published a series of Bible lessons. In addition, a number of his sermons, poetic verse, and tributes appeared in tract form. Countless articles and book reviews were accepted for publication by a host of journals. This brief annotated bibliography provides an alphabetic listing of works that have been published in book form.

"Calvary and the Empty Tomb" in *If I Had Only One Sermon to Preach,* Ralph G. Turnbull, ed. Grand Rapids, MI: Baker Book House, 1966. This Easter sermon was designed to show the depth and effective power of God's love.

Conquering the Unconquerable. Louisville, KY: The Herald Press [1948]. 138 pp. This book is designed to be a practical guide for Christian living.

Delighting in the Lord: A Biographic Sketch, with featured messages of Elizabeth Morrison (Aunt Bettie), compiled with John Paul. Louisville, KY: Pentecostal Publishing Company, 1944. 29 pp. This booklet is a short biography of the third wife of Henry Clay Morrison, founder of Asbury Theological Seminary.

The Epistles to the Corinthians. Grand Rapids, MI: Baker Book House, 1964. 154 pp. This exegetical commentary is part of the "Proclaiming the New Testament" series.

"Final Salvation and Its Concomitants" in the *The Word and the Doctrine: Studies in Contemporary Wesleyan-Arminian Theology.* Kenneth E. Geiger, comp. Kansas City, MO: Beacon Hill Press, 1965, pp. 229-235. This short study is an articulation of the Wesleyan view of the perseverance of the saints.

Faith for Men in Arms. Louisville, KY: The Herald Press [1944]. 86 pp. This booklet is designed to give guidance to those who were called to serve in the armed forces during World War II.

From Cod Fishing to Soul Fishing: A Saga of Faith. Wilmore, KY: Asbury Seminary Press, 1967. 40 pp. This booklet is based on the life of Wesley Oaks, a minister in the United Church of Canada.

The Greatest Prayer Ever Prayed. Louisville, KY: The Pentecoastal Publishing Company [1950]. 60 pp. This is a commentary on Christ's high priestly prayer recorded in John 17.

John Wesley's Heart-Warming Religion. Louisville, KY: Pentecostal Publishing Company, 1954. 64 pp. This is a discussion of the doctrine of entire sanctification based on a reflection of John Wesley's experience and writings.

The Life Story of Lizzie H. Glide. San Francisco, CA: Eagle Printing Company, 1936. 107 pp. This biography is of the life of the person who financed the construction of the Glide Memorial Methodist Church in San Francisco where the author pastored for many years.

The Power that Prevails. Louisville, KY: Pentecostal Publishing Company, 1938. 156 pp. Abridged as Power for You. Louisville, KY: Pentecostal Publishing Company, 1940. 71 pp. This discussion of the doctrine of entire santification is expressed in the spirit baptism motifs of Luke-Acts.

Prayer: The Most Powerful Force in the World. Louisville, KY: The Herald Press 1950. As the title implies, this is a discussion of the nature of prayer.

Religious Trends Today, Louisville, KY: The Herald Press, 1938. 54 pp. This booklet treats such topics as zionism, anti-Semitism, atheism, communism, pacifism, capitalism, temperance, evangelism and missions.

"The Sanctification of J. C. McPheeters" in *Flames of Living Fire: Testimonies to the Experience of Entire Sanctification.* Bernie Smith, ed. Kansas City, MO: Beacon Hill Press, 1950. This is Dr. McPheeters' personal testimony.

Sons of God. Upland, IN: Taylor University Press, 1929. 211 pp. This book of sermons on a number of topics was the author's first book.

Sunshine and Victory. Nashville, TN: Cokesbury Press, 1933. 121 pp. Reprinted in abridged form under the same title by The Pentecostal Publishing Company, 1940. 64 pp. This is an autobiographical sketch focusing on his battle with and deliverance from tuberculosis.

---

*It should be noted that the personal papers of Dr. J. C. McPheeters have been deposited in the Asbury Theological Seminary Archives.

About the Author

Chilton McPheeters grew up in a Methodist parsonage, the son of Dr. J. C. McPheeters. He is married and the father of three children. He holds an A.B. in history from the University of California in Berkeley, a B.D. from Asbury Theological Seminary, and a Ph.D. from Drew University with a major in theology and philosophy of religion.

He has pastored churches in Kentucky, New Jersey, Connecticut, New York, California and Arizona. A Navy Chaplain during WW II, he spent most of his time with the Marines. He was one time Director of Christian Education for the Queens Federation of Churches, New York City, and adjunct professor at Hofstra University, Long Island University, New York University, Azusa Pacific College and Fuller Theological Seminary. He has also served as a District Superintendent.

Chilton McPheeters has been involved in summer evangelism and pioneer pulpit exchange programs in Japan and Korea. For twenty-five years he was editor of a weekly parish column, "Chilt Chats," with a national readership. He served on the General Conference Commission on Worship, and was past delegate to General and Jurisdictional Conferences. He was also a participant in Faith and Order, Oxford Theological Institute, colloquy on "The Loss and Recovery of the Sacred." He has been active in programs of evangelism and church renewal, and has traveled widely, including five study seminar trips to the Holy Land and Europe.